The Bard Unbarred

Alan Blunden

With thanks to my family and members of the Harlow Writers, who gave me so much encouragement.

'I beseech your Grace, pardon me. I was born to speak all mirth and no matter.' (Much Ado about Nothing)

Published by ACB Publishing. CM23 3NP.
a.blunden@talktalk.net
Copyright © Alan Blunden 2016

Cover and artwork by End Associates
nick@endassociates.co.uk

ISBN 978-0-9955234-0-1

Contents

The History Plays

The Comedies

The Tragedies

The Romances

Introduction

The man from Stratford-on-Avon: use those words anywhere in the world and people will know you are referring to William Shakespeare.

So what is it about this writer and why are his plays still as popular as ever, four hundred years after his death?

The most quoted and quotable writer of all time and an inspiration to future generations of writers and poets, his plays are still being performed all over the world.

Many have been turned into films, musicals and ballets.

A remarkable fact when you consider that the plot for almost every play was not his own.

Many have said that being taught Shakespeare at school turned them off. And it is true that sometimes the language can be impenetrable.

I hope that by writing these synopses in a slightly humorous vein, I have been able to make his works more accessible.

I feel it would be unjust to finish this introduction without giving mention to John Hemminge and Henry Condell.

Without the efforts of these two friends: both actors and friends of Shakespeare, it is likely that many of his plays would have been lost.

Left a small sum of money in his will, they spent the seven years following his death, gathering together all the quartos, folios, scraps of paper etc., before putting them into the First Folio.

I hope you enjoy reading these synopses as much as I've enjoyed writing them. I also hope they will provide an insight into the wonderful and varied characters given life by the man from Stratford-on-Avon.

The History Plays

The tragic History of King Richard the Second

The story of a young man who,
Was known to all as Richard Two.
The play begins with two young gents,
Wrapped in a heated argument.
The air is filled with much abuse,
As each the other doth accuse.

'Tom Mowbray is a dodgy bloke,'
Says John Gaunt's son: young Bolingbroke.
'This man,' he tells the youthful king,
'Has done a really horrid thing.
'T would not,' he says, 'be too unkind,
To say this man has robbed you blind.
And furthermore, I tell you true,
He wants to kill my uncle too.'

Tom Mowbray, who's the Norfolk duke,
Gives Bolingbroke a strong rebuke.
But after hearing each one out,
King Richard Two has little doubt,
That both are equally to blame,
And thus should suffer equal shame.

Says Richard, who is England's head,
'The two of you are banishéd.'
Mowbray, the cause of all the strife,
Is sentenced to a term of life.

While Bolingbroke, now close to tears,
Is banned from England for ten years.
When John of Gaunt; Bolingbroke's dad,
Hears the news he is hopping mad.

He tells the king, 'I think you're bent
And rubbish at good government.'

Once having got that off his chest,
He then goes to his final rest.
With John Gaunt dead, quick as a flash,
King Richard swoops and grabs his cash.
Which leaves the banished Bolingbroke,
Bereft, alone and stony broke.

With cash galore King Richard goes
To Ireland, to put down his foes.
His uncle, Duke of York, will stay,
To rule the realm while he's away.
As it turns out a big mistake:
The sort young people often make.

No sooner has he left the shore,
Than Bolingbroke comes back once more.
Old York is now somewhat concerned,
And asks him why he has returned.
Though York's not sure exactly what,
He thinks he has in mind a plot.

Says Bolingbroke; his eyes alight,
'I only want what's mine by right.
That's the reason and nothing more,
Why I've returned to England's shore.
The mighty army that you see,
Is there to keep me company.'

When Richard comes back home once more,
He wonders what he came back for.
His uncle's joined with Bolingbroke.
He's hated by the common folk.
The Welsh have left him on his own.
How will he ever keep the throne?

He knows full well he's in a hole

And gives back all the cash he stole.
Young Bolingbroke, his erstwhile friend,
Is told his exile now can end.
All it seems is hunky-dory.
But there's much more to the story.

Things now are getting Richard down.
It seems the whole world wants his crown.
His cousin Aumerle; naughty thing,
Has done the Duke of Gloucester in.
Or so the accusation goes.
If true or not nobody knows.

It's now that Bolingbroke steps in
And has himself crowned as the king.
Thus Richard; left without a mate,
Decides it's time to abdicate.
But in the court, as said before,
There are plotters by the score.

A group of malcontented men
Wants Richard on the throne again.
Among them Aumerle, old York's son,
Who wants to see it quickly done.
But he himself is swiftly caught.
Then brought before the royal court.

Instead of ending up deceased,
Aumerle's forgiven, then released!
But for the one-time mighty king,
The knell of doom begins to ring.
In Pomfret castle locked away,
Down on his knees he starts to pray

That just like Aumerle he will be,
Forgiven and shown clemency.
But while he's banged up in his cell,
The king does not behave too well.
He gets into a brawling fight

And kills two servants out of spite.

But ere he can kill any more,
He too is beaten to the floor.
The news of Richard's swift demise,
Brings tears into the new king's eyes.
(It's not that strange if we recall:
He was his cousin after all!)

And so we reach the final part.
Where Bolingbroke, with heavy heart,
Attempts his feelings to assuage,
By going on a pilgrimage.
Of him of course we'll hear much more,
In Part the First of Henry Four.

Henry the Fourth-Part One

As he prepares for pilgrimage unto the Holy Land,
King Henry hears the news that things have not gone quite as
planned.
His scheme to put the Welsh folk down has run in to a wall.
And now the rebel, Glendower, has Mortimer in thrall.

Far better news from up north comes, where Hotspur's in the field.
And many troublous Scottish lords have now been forced to yield.
Though glad to hear of victory, the King still has the blues.
While Hotspur fights for England, his own son is on the booze.

Not for Hal the battlefield that could mean an early grave.
He'd sooner be in Eastcheap with Jack Falstaff, rascally knave.
Where with Peto, Poins and Bardolph: all villains to a man.
He's busy quaffing pints of ale and hatching out a plan.

They plot a crafty subterfuge with Falstaff at its heart.
To carry out a hold up, in which each will play a part.
But Poins and Hal together then devise a better wheeze,
They hope will bring the boastful Falstaff crashing to his knees.

In the meantime, back at court, there is friction in the air.
As Worcester and Northumberland are not too keen to share
The Scottish lords they captured: all nobles of renown,
With Henry Four of England, current holder of the crown.

To them he seems ungrateful and does nothing else but moan.
About the very people helped to put him on the throne.
They plan to rise against him and to rob him of his power,
By throwing in their lot with Douglas and the great Glendower.

In a wood near Rochester, at the appointed date,

Falstaff and his cronies meet and there they lie in wait.
Prince Hal and Poins then hide away until the deed is done.
Now is the time for Hal and Poins to have a little fun.

The jokers then both reappear, each wearing a disguise.
Thus taking Jack and all his pals completely by surprise.
They rob him of the cash he stole, which gives him such a fright.
That in the twinkling of an eye he disappears from sight.

Later, at the Boar's Head Inn, there is banter all around.
When a Sheriff comes looking for a thief who's large and round.
Full of fear and apprehension, Jack Falstaff hides from sight.
Prince Hal then tells the Sheriff, he himself will put things right.

And so the fun continues, till long into the day.
As Jack and Hal together perform a little play.
Both loaded to the gunnels with quantities of sack,
Jack takes on the part of king and Hal the part of Jack.

But then there comes a message from King Henry to his son.
'Return,' the message tells him, 'there is much work to be done.'
But while the king's rebuking Hal, a parley's taking place,
Twixt Mortimer and Hotspur, who are meeting face to face

With Worcester and Glendower, they're hatching out a plan,
To push King Henry off the throne as quickly as they can.
This done they'll then divide the land in equal parts of three.
But Hotspur is not satisfied, he simply can't agree.

Though he'll be given all the land from Trent up to the Tweed,
Hotspur feels it's not enough, but the rest will not concede.
Severely chastened by his pa, Prince Hal now sees the light.
No more will he a wastrel be: he's up now for the fight.

He has at hand a host of men trained in the art of war
And gives Jack Falstaff cash in hand to find him many more.

Jack Falstaff goes recruiting up and down this happy land;
Returning some days later with a ragged, motley band

Of bumpkins, idlers, ne'er-do-wells, for whom the Prince has paid.
Though crafty Jack assures him that they all will make the grade.
They then march on to Shrewsbury, where at the fateful hour,
They'll meet with Harry Hotspur, with Earl Douglas and Glendower.

Deep in the heat of battle, with no end it seems in sight,
Earl Douglas threatens Henry Four and gives him quite a fright.
Things are looking very bad; the king's race is almost run.
But then he's rescued by Prince Hal, his erstwhile wayward son.

The battle rages on and on... who will the victor be?
And what of Falstaff, lying stunned, beneath an ancient tree?
When he awakes and looks around, there on the ground close by,
The corpse of Harry Hotspur, with an arrow in his eye.

Quick-thinking Falstaff scoops him up and carries him away.
'T was I,' he claims, 'killed Harry Hotspur, earlier today.'
(In truth it was Prince Hal who'd laid young Harry Hotspur low.
A fact the wily Falstaff oh so plainly does not know)

Now Harry Hotspur's popped his clogs his mates are in a hole.
Each one will be dismembered and his head stuck on a pole.
Farewell to Harry Hotspur and to Worcester his great friend,
To Vernon and to Blunt - a royal stalwart to the end.

Though the battle now is over; the war has not been won.
There's still a lot that needs be done by Henry and his son.
Glendower and Northumberland their struggle will renew.
We'll find out what becomes of them in Henry Four Part Two.

Henry the Fourth Part Two

False Rumour tells Northumberland,
That Harry Hotspur and his band,
Have beaten Henry and his son.
'They have,' he says, 'the battle won.'
But rumour, as the name implies,
Has told the earl a pack of lies.
As later on the truth's revealed.
His young son Hotspur's in a field.
Dead as a doornail; passed away...
'T was Henry Four who'd won the day!

Meanwhile in Eastcheap sly old Jack,
Is busy downing quarts of sack.
But now he has a brand new pal:
A pageboy given by Prince Hal.
Who tells the knight, 'Your sampled pee
Appears much healthier than thee.'

Meanwhile rebellion's in the air,
As Scroop and other lords prepare,
To wage a most illegal war,
Against the ailing Henry Four.
Whose troops are split twixt Wales and France.
Which makes them think they have a chance.

Archbishop Scroop and Hastings think,
They'll push King Henry to the brink.
With help from Bardolph* and Mowbray,
(*A lord of rank and high estate,
And not the one who's Falstaff's mate.)
They feel that they can win the day.
And though Northumberland's a doubt,

They still think they're in with a shout.

Meanwhile at lowly Boar's Head Inn,
There is a most unholy din.
As sheriff Fang and sheriff Snare,
Confront Jack Falstaff in his lair,
Demanding payment of his bills.
And then to add more to his ills,
The Lord Chief Justice comes along,
Accusing him of doing wrong.

'It is,' he says, 'quite plain to me,
That you took part in robbery.
And furthermore, I'd have to say,
You've led the young Prince Hal astray.'
But with a false tear in his eye,
Jack Falstaff doth each charge deny.

Instead of boozing at The Boar.
Jack should be getting fit for war.
But there's a girl who lights his fire:
Who fills his heart with great desire.
Mistress Quickly, who owns the inn,
That Jack does all his drinking in.
'T is she who keeps the old rogue fed.
And she's the one he says he'll wed.

Meanwhile the old king's feeling sick.
Which cuts the young prince to the quick.
And after some light badinage,
Exchange of wit and persiflage,
With Poins, Bardolph and tubby Jack,
Prince Hal decides to hurry back
To cheer his dad, who's been ground down
By years of wearing England's crown.

And then Jack Falstaff's off again,
To find the king some fighting men.
In Gloucestershire, which lies far west.

He puts five yokels to the test.
All five unlikely candidates,
Presented by his erstwhile mates,
Shallow and Silence two JP's,
Who both are very keen to please.

First there's Mouldy, who's less than bold,
Because he has an awful cold.
Shadow, Feeble, Bullcalf and Wart:
A motley crew of lowly sort.
Bullcalf and Mouldy pay a fee,
For which Jack Falstaff sets them free.
Thus, ill prepared for what's in store,
The other three march off to war.

Lord Mowbray and Archbishop York,
Meet once again to talk the talk
With Hastings and to hatch a plan,
To blow away the sickly man.
And once the King is overthrown,
To put their own man on the throne.
But then comes news that makes it plain,
Northumberland has fled again.

This time to Scotland out of sight,
Where he will wait while others fight.
And once the bloody battle's done,
He'll join whichever side has won.

But then it seems a stroke of luck.
Before a single blow is struck
Prince John, the third in line appears.
He seeks to calm the rebels' fears.
By telling them their sovereign lord,
Has sworn by God and given word
That he's forgiven everyone.
They shake and so the deal is done.

An act for which they pay the price,

For John's as false as loaded dice...
He goes back on the oath he swore,
And soon the rebels are no more.
With Hastings, York and Mowbray down,
He goes back home to London town.
Where brother Hal and portly Jack,
Are busy drinking yet more sack.

Which causes Henry great concern,
And brings on one more funny turn.
It's one of many, many strokes,
From which he very nearly croaks!
When Hal returns his dad's abed,
The crown of state beside his head.
Hal takes it up from where it lies
And tries it on himself for size.

When Henry sees what Hal has done,
He reprimands his wayward son.
But there's little argufying,
As it's clear the king is dying.
But Hal of course, who's still alive,
Will soon be crowned as Henry Five.
Westminster Abbey is the place,
He'll get the sceptre, orb and mace.

Emboldened by the news fat Jack,
Puts down his glass and hurries back.
And joins in as the crowds applaud
King Henry Five, their sovereign lord.
From deep within the throng he cries,
'It's me, fat Jack, surprise, surprise.'
Surprise for Jack, but not for Hal,
Who used to be his bosom pal.

For while the crown sits on his pate,
Hal can no longer be his mate.
Now he's the king the die is cast.
Their boozing days are in the past.

There'll be no more of cakes and ale,
As Jack and pals end up in jail.

Henry the Sixth Part One

Alack, alack, alack a day.
King Henry Five has passed away.
So who will rule now in his stead?
And wear the crown upon his head?
And who is waiting in the wings,
To occupy the throne of kings?

The answer is a nine-month child, still wet behind the ears.
But can the country e'er be ruled, by one so young in years?
Especially when the French abroad are playing up so much.
The country badly needs a man who has the common touch.

By happenstance there are two men; both have a good CV.
Humphrey, Duke of Gloucester and Henry Beaufort from the see
Of Winchester, where he as bishop served for many years.
So he and Humphrey now will strive to calm the country's fears.

In France the wars against the French are going down the pan.
The French have found a girl who fights and dresses like a man.
The Frenchmen call her La Poucelle; the English, Joan of Arc.
And in the briefest spell of time this lady makes her mark.

She drives the English from Orleans and sends them on their way.
For which the English, led by Talbot, swear to make her pay.
Beneath a moonless, starless sky the Englishmen attack.
They beat the Frenchmen out of sight and take Orleans back.

The Countess of Auvergne attempts great Talbot to beguile.
But he is far too clever to be tempted by her smile.
He has a mind to vandalise and dominate the French.
He has no time to fraternise, though she's a comely wench.

In England's green and pleasant land, the home of liberty,
The two men who are now in charge begin to disagree.
Outside the Tower of London, the couple start to fight.
On seeing this the Mayor of London tries to put things right.

He finally convinces them to be the best of friends.
But being mates with Humphrey's not what Winchester intends.
Meanwhile in Temple Gardens scarce a mile or so apart,
A game of picking roses is just about to start.

Richard of York and Somerset set others there a test.
To pick the white rose then the red, and say which one is best.
The red rose stands for Lancaster; the white rose stands for York.
The choosing of the red or white will end the need for talk.

Some go for roses that are white, while some go for the red.
This choosing of the roses signals trouble is ahead.
Before his uncle, Mortimer, lays down his head to die,
He tells his nephew, Richard, to keep a watchful eye.

'To claim the throne of England, which by rights belong to you.'
'Be politic,' he tells him, 'in most everything you do.'

Rouen meanwhile has fallen to the doughty La Poucelle.
(For one still in her teenage years this girl has done quite well!)
A sad, sad day for England; things are looking pretty black.
But with the aid of Burgundy great Talbot takes it back.

But Burgundy's a dirty rat; a traitor through and through.
He tells the Maid of Orleans, 'I'd rather be with you.'
On hearing of this treachery King Henry blows his top.
And Talbot is commissioned to give Burgundy the chop.

Meanwhile in Merrie England the Roses red and white,
Are falling out repeatedly and spoiling for a fight.
The upshot of this contretemps is awful to relate.
No troops are sent across to France, thus sealing Talbot's fate.

Now Talbot and his son are dead, Joan sees this as a chance

To drive the hated Englishmen from her beloved France.
'Please help,' she asks the spirits, 'give the Dauphin back his crown.'
But they are in a rotten mood and turn the poor girl down.

She loses out to Gloucester, (This girl cannot get a break!)
And though she pleads for clemency, they burn her at the stake.
There is another problem for King Henry to address.
To foster good relations, he must find a French Princess.

The Earl of Suffolk has the answer… Margaret of Anjou.
'I recommend this lass,' he says, 'she'll be so good for you.'

This gesture's not so generous as first it might appear.
He hopes the lovely lady will King Henry domineer.
That he'll shower him with favours, he thinks are overdue.
But more about this evil man in Henry Six Part Two.

Henry the Sixth Part Two

The palace is the opening scene,
Where Henry welcomes his new queen.
Says he,' Fair Margaret of Anjou,
This loving kiss is just for you.'

It seems at first a perfect match,
But there's a snag, which doth attach.
Before the wedding can take place,
There are conditions he must face.

For ere she gives her dainty hand,
The king must give up bits of land.
Anjou and Maine just for a start,
Are realms with which the king must part.

An option, which by Henry's peers,
Is greeted with repeated jeers.

The Duke of Gloucester and Beaufort still can't see eye to eye.
The acrimony twixt the pair grows more as time goes by.
The Duke of York, Plantagenet, is waiting for a chance,
To seize the throne as well as being regent of all France.

Skulduggery and intrigue is the order of the day.
The common folk of England also want to have their say.
Peter Thump, Tom Horner's aide, his master doth accuse,
Of sedition, chicanery and having impure views.

He tells the court his master thinks that York should be the king.
An ill-considered point of view, for which the man could swing.
The court agrees and tells him it's a thing to be abhorred.

On hearing this young Peter Thump puts Horner to the sword.

Gloucester's wife's ambitions now come quickly to the fore.
She asks a priest to find out what the future has in store.
Caught by Buckingham and York, brought before her sovereign lord.
Where he; though weak as water, sends the hapless girl abroad.

For the wifeless Duke of Gloucester, things go from bad to worse.
His foes have just one thing in mind... to see him in a hearse.
Suffolk, Beaufort, the queen and York heap charges on his head.
And though he's uncle to the king, poor Gloucester soon is dead.

Being too close to royalty is really not much fun.
And many more will kick the bucket ere the play is done.
Suffolk: lover of the queen, is the next to disappear.
Chopped down while he's in exile by a scurvy buccaneer.

Angered by corruption and by the taxes they must pay.
The discontent of common folk increases day on day.
From out this seething turbulence of hate and discontent.
A mob sets off to London to confront the government.

Led by a fellow called Jack Cade, who claims the English throne.
The mob kills several lords and knights, before Jack's overthrown.
From Ireland meanwhile York returns, his army close at hand.
He plans to kick out Somerset, a man he cannot stand.

To keep him safe from wrathful York and his army at bay,
Henry locks up Somerset and then throws the key away.
With Somerset in prison, the Duke of York's contented.
A lot of argy-bargy and bloodshed's been prevented.

But there is yet another twist as Henry changes tack.
Somerset is freed from jail and then warmly welcomed back.
It's all too much for York and Warwick, Salisbury and the rest.
And soon there is a battle royal to find out who is best.

St. Albans is the battle site in fourteen fifty-five.
The red rose pitched against the white, but which one will survive?

The Duke of York slays Clifford, who is Henry's greatest friend.
York's son, Richard, kills Somerset, before the battle's end.
King Henry knows the game is up and flies off like a bird.
We'll find out what becomes of him in Henry part the third.

Henry the Sixth Part Three

With Lord Clifford among the dead,
King Henry's from the battle fled
To London, but when he gets there,
He finds that York is in his chair.

York says he'll leave the king alone,
And give him back the royal throne,
But only on condition he
Will leave it to his family.
The weak and feeble king agrees.
(There's nothing he won't do to please.)

His spouse, Queen Margaret's not so mild.
She wants it left to their own child:
The Prince of Wales and rightful heir
To sceptre, orb and royal chair.

The sons of York berate their pa.
They see it as a step too far.
They make their feelings very plain.
And urge him to go back again.

Bombarded with their constant rage,
The Duke's no choice but to renege.
Then with his army close behind.
He tells the king he's changed his mind.

He then adopts a threatening tone;
Informing him he wants the throne.
Which pleases not King Henry's wife,
Who tells the Duke, 'not on your life.'

They meet at Wakefield in the Dales.
The Duke attempts but sadly fails,
To beat Queen Margaret in the fray.
For she it is who wins the day.

Edmund, son of York is slaughtered.
York himself is somewhat altered.
The queen and Clifford stab him dead.
And then cut off the poor chap's head.

The fight continues at a pace.
As Warwick's next to face disgrace.
He's beaten by the warlike queen.
And quickly flees the battle scene.

Giving in is a heinous sin.
But Warwick thinks he still can win.
And so the battle's joined again.
And though she struggles might and main,
Watched by the weak and feeble king,
She does her best but fails to win.

And then without a backward glance,
She grabs her son and flees to France.
With Margaret gone, bereft of power,
The king is locked up in the tower.
And with the poor Lord Clifford dead,
The white rose overpowers the red.

Because old York is six feet down,
His young son Edward dons the crown.
With Margaret by him as his queen,
With just a little gap between.
Edward the Fourth he now will be.
And reign till fourteen eighty-three.

The Earl of Warwick then decides,
It's time that Edward had a bride.
He sees this as a golden chance,

To form a union with France.
'I think it's time,' he tells young Ted,
'For you to share a wedding bed.'

He says he knows a comely wench,
Who's young and beautiful... and French.
The lady that he has in mind,
Is of a very special kind.
Who by the purest happenstance,
Is daughter to the King of France.

But Warwick's plans are blown away,
When Edward falls for Lady Grey.
The king has chosen as his bride,
A girl who backs the other side!
She's Lancastrian born and bred.
So is it right that they should wed?

His trip to France now deemed a flop,
The Earl of Warwick blows his top.
He wants to see Ted overthrown
And give King Henry back the throne.

Possession of the throne it seems brings out the worst in men.
As the Yorkists and Lancastrians go to war again.
Edward's brother, Duke of Gloucester, a sly and slippery thing,
Wants to see his brother dead and himself proclaimed as king.

Warwick and Queen Margaret, aided by the king of France,
Assemble a great army, then to England they advance.
Warwick offers up his daughter to Edward, Margaret's son.
They then set sail to England, once the marriage deal is done.

But in this sceptred, sea-girt isle, the discontent is rife.
The populace is not too pleased with Edward's choice of wife.
Duke Clarence, Edward's brother, crosses to the other side.
Where Warwick gives his youngest girl to be his blushing bride.

Crookback Richard, Duke of Gloucester, stands by his brother Ted.

Though deep inside his evil soul he'd like to see him dead.
Warwick's men land in England and free Henry from the jail.
But the noble lord's intentions are doomed alas to fail.

Poor Henry's sick of sitting with the crown upon his head.
So Warwick and Duke Clarence jointly rule the land instead.
King Edward, helped by Crookback Dick, escapes to Burgundy.
Once there they raise an army then sail back across the sea.

They capture feeble Henry and they lock him up again.
Which signals the beginning of another dire campaign.
The scene moves on to Coventry where Warwick lies in wait.
But he and his great army will soon meet an awful fate.

Meanwhile the fickle Clarence has another change of heart.
And goes back to his brother, vowing never more to part.
Then Margaret comes with warlike horde of thirty thousand men
To fight at Tewksbury in the west, but sadly fails again.

She is beaten to a frazzle by Edward's merry band.
Her son is killed and she herself is banished from the land.
Gloucester goes to London town and stabs poor Henry dead.
The crown of England's placed once more on Yorkist Edward's head.

Richard the Third.

It is the twenty-first of May.
And Henry Six has passed away.
Among the mourners, Lady Anne:
A dowager without a man.
King Henry was her pa-in-law.
For her the outlook's pretty poor

She has no husband or a child nor boyfriend on the go.
Sweet Lady Anne the dowager is feeling pretty low.
Not bothered by the fact she's grieving for the loss of life,
The Duke of Gloucester, son of York, asks her to be his wife.

It's an awkward situation that puts her on the spot.
But in the end she acquiesces, then they tie the knot.
The marriage done and dusted, Richard leaves the wedding bower,
To concentrate on Clarence, who is locked up in the tower.

Though Clarence is his brother, he's in Richard's scheming way.
An awkward situation for which soon he'll have to pay.
For Richard has one aim in life: one goal and one alone.
He has his beady, evil eye, fixed firmly on the throne.

As history records it, Clarence liked a little drink.
A practice, which he carried on whilst still locked up in clink.
But Clarence is the sort of chap who's never toed the line.
So Richard has him dumped into a butt of Malmsey wine.

His other brother, Edward Four, is current head of state.
Though sadly he's a sickly man, whose chances aren't that great.
While his ailing older brother is tucked up tight in bed,
Assisted by Lord Hastings, Richard rules in Edward's stead.

With the help of Buckingham and the Mayor of London Town,
Cruel Richard is now very close to capturing the crown.
When Edward dies he leaves behind two boys as natural heirs.
But Richard is determined that the crown shall not be theirs.

Ere either of the dead king's sons can take the reins of power,
Quick thinking Richard has them locked up in the bloody tower.
The crown will never sit upon the top of either head.
As in a very little while, the princes both are dead.

The world is Richard's oyster now; he's reached the very top.
But no such luck for Hastings... that poor fellow gets the chop.
The late king's wife, Elizabeth, is filled with mortal fear.
And with the kids from her first marriage quickly disappears.

Convinced that Richard's guilty of the princes' swift demise,
The bold young Duke of Buckingham straight to the palace flies.
With quite outstanding arrogance, he says unto the king.
'You're a very naughty boy; you've done the princes in.

But I'll keep quiet if you give me an earldom straight away.'
A foolish proposition and a dangerous game to play.
Richard waves the threat aside, giving Buckingham short shrift.
And from then on between the two there is a widening rift.

His head still in its proper place, Duke Buckingham departs,
To find some men to fight the king...it's now the trouble starts.
He tries to raise an army but the venture is a flop.
And just like poor old Hastings, he eventually gets the chop.

King Richard who has lost his wife; the lovely Lady Anne.
Is seeking to replace her just as quickly as he can.
He wants the young Elizabeth to be his blushing bride.
(The daughter of his brother who only recently has died!)

Henry Tudor, Earl of Richmond, a claimant to the crown,
Resolves to set the record straight and take King Richard down.
With his army gathered round him, they meet at Bosworth Field.
Where, on the bloody battleground, King Richard's fate is sealed.

With Richard dead, the Roses' wars have reached a natural end.
And the victor; saintly Richmond, sets out to make amends.
He plans to wed that lovely lass: the late King Richard's niece.
And rule as Henry Seven in a realm of blessed peace.

Henry the Fifth

Alack, alack, alack a day,
King Henry Four has had his day.
He's kicked the bucket, poor old thing,
Now Henry Five will be the king.
A lad who is to tell the truth,
A wild and somewhat reckless youth,
Who often at the Boar's Head drank,
With fellows of much lower rank.
Pistol, Nim and Bardolph too,
With whom he shared a jug or two.
But now he has affairs of state,
On which he needs to concentrate.
For after years of discontent,
The country needs good government.

Now that he's king he'll have a chance,
To press his claim to rule in France.
Thus, to the Dauphin he makes known,
That he intends to take his throne.
Which the Dauphin so much appals,
That he responds with tennis balls.
An insult that makes Henry sore,
And sets him on the road to war.
The common folk throughout the land,
Are keen to join with Henry's band.
Though reluctant Bardolph and Nim,
And Pistol too unite with him,
To fight against the common foe.
But there's delay before they go.

The Earl of Cambridge Scroop and Grey,

Have planned to spoil King Henry's day.
Each thinking he would never know,
They'd passed on secrets to the foe.
But once their evil plot's revealed,
The fate of all three men is sealed.
And when their guilt is fully proved,
Each plotter has his head removed.
This done King Henry sets to sea.
And soon he reaches Normandy.

His army marches through the land creating quite a stir.
Till they reach the battlements of a town they call Harfleur.
'Lay down your weapons,' cries the king. 'I am your sovereign liege.'
'No way,' reply the residents, and thus begins a siege.

For five long weeks the town holds out, but finally gives in.
And hands the key to Henry Five, who'll be their sovereign king.
With Harfleur in his pocket now the king moves on apace.
But on the way a deed is done, which brings with it disgrace.
Bardolph and Nim steal from a church, which angers their great king.
And he, with lack of charity, condemns the pair to swing.

At Agincourt the French await.
They hope to seal King Henry's fate.
But first they send brave Montjoy to
Tell Henry what he ought to do.
The herald says, 'we're five to one.
The best thing you can do is run.'
But Henry treats his words with scorn,
And so the battle lines are drawn.

The night before the bloody fray,
King Henry makes his sombre way,
Dressed up in clothes to look like them,
Among his bold but worried men.
Fluellen, Williams, Bates and Court,
And common men of every sort.
He listens to their hopes and fears,

Before the morning sun appears.

The battle rages to and fro.
And then the final overthrow...
England has won. The French have lost.
And now it's time to count the cost.
The French have suffered greater pain.
Ten thousand of them now lay slain.
Among them knights of great renown,
By England's archers stricken down.

The king of France old Charlie Six,
Now finds he's in an awful fix.
He has a daughter, Katherine,
Who Henry wants to be his queen.
So he and Charles negotiate,
For Katherine to be his mate.

Young Kate agrees to be his bride.
And thus both lands are unified.

King Henry the Eighth

Says Prologue, 'woe and yet more woe,
I think you really ought to know.
This play that we present to thee,
Is filled with death and misery.'

Though it seems there's not a reason,
Buckingham's accused of treason.
(He tried to nail the Cardinal;
King Henry's confidant and pal.
But then discovered, far too late,
You never slag off Henry's mate.)
Queen Catherine who is Henry's wife,
Does all she can to save his life.
And though she goes on bended knee,
The king ignores her urgent plea.

A maid in waiting, Anne Boleyn,
Has caught the eye of England's king.
Though Catherine for years has been,
A loyal and a faithful queen,
She's failed to give the king a son.
Which means the poor girl's race is run.

A dispensation from the Pope,
Is Henry's one and only hope.
Thus, Wolsey and his sovereign lord,
Seek counsel from the church abroad.
Together then they plan a course,
To bring about a quick divorce.

'Perforce,' the Catholic Church replies,

'You're married till your missus dies.'
And even though it's deemed a sin,
He marries mistress Anne Boleyn.
Which puts poor Wolsey in a whirl.
He'd had in mind another girl

To be King Henry's blushing bride.
Who would mayhap with luck provide,
A bonny, bouncing baby boy
And bring the king much longed for joy.
But now of course there's not a chance,
He'll ever wed this girl from France.

But things then go from bad to worse.
As Wolsey's luck goes in reverse.
A letter falls in Henry's hands,
With details of all Wolsey's lands;
Wealth, possessions, expensive things,
Which total more than his - the king's.

Having all this unknown wealth
Is very bad for Wolsey's health.
Thus, this man who's greatly hated,
Has his goodies confiscated.

And now with Wolsey in disgrace,
Sir Thomas More will take his place.
And Thomas Cranmer soon will be,
Archbishop of old Canterbury.
To Leicester then poor Wolsey flies,
And of the dreaded lurgy dies.

When Catherine hears of Wolsey's death,
She's not that sad but nonetheless,
She listens with due deference,
As Griffiths speaks in his defence.
Soon after which the erstwhile queen,
Bids life farewell and leaves the scene.

Anne is pregnant: a cause for joy.
But will the baby be a boy?
The king and others wait to see,
What sex the newborn child will be.
But after hours and hours of strain,
His progeny's a girl again.

The girl is named Elizabeth,
Who later, after Mary's death,
Will dominate the royal scene.
And rule as England's virgin queen.

King John

'You must give up your lands in France, for this is our decree.
The crown belongs to Arthur; you must hand it down to he.'
So says the French ambassador, whose name is Chatillon.
'Not a chance,' says John the King, then tells him, 'get thee gone.'

The brothers Faulconbridge meanwhile are standing toe to toe,
Disputing who's the rightful heir to all their father's dough.
For Philip is a bastard; he is not his father's son.
His proper dad's the former ruler, Richard Number One.

King John suggests a clever plan he hopes will put things right.
'If you give up your claim,' he says, 'you could become a knight.
You'd have a suit of armour and a big, long pointy lance.'
Phil agrees. The deal is done. They then set sail for France.

The King of France helped by Limoges then sets about Angiers,
But stops to parley for a while when John the King appears.
They chew the cud a little while, before they go to war.
And though they struggle manfully, the outcome is a draw.

'We'll have a better chance,' says Philip, 'if we fight as one.'
Hubert de Burgh does not concur, he thinks it would be fun,
If the Dauphin, the eldest son of France's present king,
Should join in holy wedlock to the niece of John the King.

But Constance; Arthur's mother, has another point of view.
She thinks the lovesick Dauphin should have better things to do.
Then to the scene comes Pandulph, from the holy Church of Rome.
'Do not,' he says, 'conjoin with John, but send that man back home.'

The visit of the pontiff leaves King Philip feeling sore.
Quite sore enough in fact to turn his thoughts again to war.

His army is defeated, his son Arthur's whisked away.
Philip the bastard slays Limoges... it's been a busy day.

By rights the crown of England should be placed on Arthur's head.
That's good enough a reason for King John to want him dead.
He tells his henchman Hubert, 'It's about time Arthur died.'
But instead of killing Arthur, he shows him where to hide.

Meanwhile the wily Pandulph has a really super plan.
He wants the Dauphin to leave France as quickly as he can.
Pandulph makes his way to England and there confronts King John.
A man who has, in his opinion, done the Church much wrong.

The youthful Dauphin, Lewis, comes to England's hostile shore,
With an army in attendance, prepared to go to war.
With the changeling lords of England now covering his back.
The young man sees no reason to call off the planned attack.

So why then are the lords of England on the Dauphin's side?
The answer to the question is that young Prince Arthur's died.
For which the irate English lords place all the blame on John.
For was it not this evil king that wanted Arthur gone?

But they are much mistaken; it was not his fault at all,
The prince died in an accident, when falling from a wall.
John tells the wily Pandulph he'll be Catholic once more.
If in return he'll stop the Dauphin knocking down his door.

Convinced that with the English lords he has sufficient might,
The Dauphin's not in listening mood, and carries on the fight.
Then from the wounded knight, Melun, the English lords find out,
That if the Dauphin wins the war he means to wipe them out.

Unsettled by the awful news, now looking pale and wan.
The changeling lords decide to leave and hurry back to John.
The Dauphin has no option but to turn around and flee.
His ships with reinforcements having foundered while at sea,

But John the King is unaware the Dauphin's done a bunk.

He lies stone dead upon the ground... poisoned by a monk.
The late King John is laid to rest with pomp and pageantry.
His son, the next in line will rule as Henry number Three.

The Comedies

The Comedy of Errors

A tale to bring bewilderment, befuddle and confuse.
About some folk from Ephesus and distant Syracuse.
In Ephesus they have a law that will not brook excuse:
A law that's aimed at anyone who comes from Syracuse.

A law that's based on enmity, in which it's plainly said.
Pay us a thousand marks right now, or we'll chop off your head.
Duke Solinus of Ephesus tells Egeon he must pay,
A thousand Marks as ransom by the ending of the day.

The Syracusan, Egeon, relates a tale of woe,
Of a shipwreck and a drowning that happened years ago.
'I had twin boys,' he tells the Duke, 'both sent to me by God.
Each a mirror of the other, like two peas in a pod.

For each I bought a servant boy, these boys were twins as well.
But when returning to my home a tragedy befell.
My wife, my son, my son's slave too, were all swept out to sea.
And now I come to seek them out, wherever they may be.'

Egeon's son, Antipholus, then comes from Syracuse,
To sniff around and see if he can ferret out some news.
Accompanied by his servant boy, a man called Dromio,
They're recognized by everyone, no matter where they go.

So why then should these strangers in a far, unfriendly land,
Be warmly greeted like old pals and shaken by the hand?
This I will try to clarify as quickly as I may,
Will Shakespeare's plot and what took place in just a single day.

Remember how I told you of the ship that ran aground?
With all its parts swept out to sea, no bodies ever found?

The truth about what happened next I'll now reveal to you.
The aforementioned were not swallowed by the ocean blue,

But picked up by a pirate ship en route to Ephesus.
A hostile land ruled by the duke; we know as Solinus.
And so dear reader as you see not one of them did drown.
They ended up in Ephesus, where since they've settled down.

And so we have two brothers... each called Antipholus.
One who resides in Syracuse and one in Ephesus.
Two lackeys, both called Dromio, which further doth confuse.
One lives in ancient Ephesus and the other Syracuse.

The rescued man, Antipholus has built himself a life.
He's settled down in Ephesus and found a lovely wife.
But when his twin Antipholus turns up from Syracuse.
Misunderstanding and confusion from then on ensues.

Though it was the rescued twin, Adriana gave her heart,
With Syracusan twin around she can't tell them apart!
Which sets in train a sequence of most comical events.
Which, though bewildering at first, eventually make sense.

Ephesian twin's arrested and then certified as mad.
Which leaves his wife Adriana feeling very sad.
The air is filled with vitriol, with anger and abuse.
As she vents her spleen on the twin... the one from Syracuse.

Thus, thinking life in Ephesus is really not much fun,
The Syracusan twin goes seeking refuge with a nun.
He runs off to an abbey where he hopes to spend the night.
The only place he feels he's safe from Adriana's spite.

Amidst these silly goings on and great tomfoolery,
Egeon is about to pay the final penalty.
As the old man passes by the holy nunnery.
The abbess asks the duke if he will kindly set him free.

The Duke can see no reason he should spare the old man's life.

But then The Abbess tells the Duke, 'I am Egeon's wife.'
Thus he rescinds the penalty; Egeon now is free.
And with his missus at his side he's happy as can be.

Coincidence and happenstance now will reign supreme.
As Antipholus of Ephesus comes on to the scene.
Adriana 's found her husband, Antipholus his twin.
Dromio his Dromio, now the party can begin.

There never was nor never will be joy in such degree.
As the cast departs the stage for a well-earned cup of tea.

The Taming of the Shrew

Baptista has two daughters, one who's sweet and one who's not.
Bianca is the youngest one and she is loved a lot.
Lucentio, Hortensio and Gremio all plan,
To woo the fair Bianca and to wed her if they can.

But Bianca may not marry before her sister Kate
Has found a man who's brave enough to be her lifelong mate.
Our Kate's a little volatile: a termagant, a shrew,
Whenever she gets in a rage, she turns the air bright blue.

Gremio and Hortensio hatch out a little plan,
To find a husband for fierce Kate as quickly as they can.
At this point I'll pause awhile, as I try to make it plain,
Why Bianca's suitors each change place… then change back again.

Lucentio swaps places with his witty serving man.
Tranio's now Lucentio and here's their cunning plan.
Lucentio, now Cambio, and as a tutor dressed,
Tries his luck with Bianca, but the lady's unimpressed.

Then to the town there comes a man, Petruchio by name.
To find a wife; a wealthy one, is young Petruchio's aim.
The man from old Verona says that he can hardly wait,
To tame the shrew of Padua, and take her as his mate.

And in spite of Kate's resistance a wedding date is made.
(Very soon the shrewish one will no longer be a maid)
Baptista is delighted, he's as happy as can be.
With Kate away once more he'll have a life of harmony.

The wedding day is over, now the loving couple kiss.
The vicar gives his blessing, so will everything be bliss?

Petruchio has his wealthy bride and now it's time to go.
The fiery Kate is unaware. How could she ever know,
That there will be no food or sleep, until she toes the line?
The poor girl's made to sit and watch, while all the others dine!

They then go home again to see the father of the bride
And bump into a stranger, as to Padua they ride.
The man they meet: Vincentio, is on his way to see
His son the young Lucentio, who's married secretly.

Bianca is the girl he's wed, and so it would appear,
Gremio and Hortensio are both out on their ear.
No problem for Hortensio, he's someone else in mind.
An ancient widow lives nearby, and she's the marrying kind.

A stranger then adopts the role of old Vincentio.
The wealthy father of the suitor; young Lucentio.
This masquerade's made to fade, when Petruchio comes to town,
And gives the vile impostor a proper dressing down.

At the house of old Baptista, a party is arranged.
It's then we find out just how much the fiery Kate has changed.
No longer is she dragon-like, disputing this and that.
The lass who was a termagant, is now a pussycat.

The two Gentlemen of Verona

Valentine and Proteus, have been mates since time began.
But then one day says Valentine, 'I'm off to old Milan.
'Then fare ye well,' says Proteus, 'but I must here abide,
For here lives fairest Julia, I plan to make my bride.'
To prove how much he loves her, he sends the lass a letter.
Which she reads then tears to bits, watched by her maid Lucetta.

Meanwhile his dad, Antonio, a most ambitious man,
Thinks his son should join his pal at the court in old Milan.
Ere he goes he says goodbye to the apple of his eye;
Exchanging rings and telling her, 'I'll love you till I die.'
And so it is that Proteus goes quickly as he can,
Followed closely by fair Julia... dressed up as a man.

But since they parted Valentine has fallen deep in love,
With a lass who's locked away in her bedroom up above.
The object of his loving thoughts is Lady Silvia,
The daughter of the duke, though Proteus also fancies her.
Then Valentine shows Proteus a ladder made from rope.
With which he hopes to rescue her and later on elope.

Quick as a flash he tells the duke what Valentine has planned,
The duke is not amused and poor old Valentine is banned.
He leaves straightway for Mantua, deceived by his old chum.
A sad, sad day for Valentine, but there is worse to come.
Whilst passing through a forest, there among the greenwood trees,
He's captured by a motley band of vagabonds and thieves.

Back in Milan, the duke has plans to see his daughter wed.
Not to the youthful Valentine, but Thurio instead.
Thurio's a good deal older, a dullard and a fool.

And hardly someone Silvia would look upon as cool.
So how to win fair Silvia and make her all his own?
The answer is a poem, with a nice, romantic tone.

But the poem gets no plaudits; in fact it's cast aside.
It's Valentine she wants to wed, and will not be denied.
Which makes it clear that Thurio is not her kind of man.
And with the help of Eglamour, she plans to leave Milan.
Meanwhile the lovely Julia comes, still dressed up as a boy
(A visit that is ill advised, and brings her little joy.)

She sees her boyfriend, Proteus, whilst down on bended knee,
Imploring with fair Silvia, 'please, please, please marry me.'
'Begone;' she tells him forcefully, 'I never will be thine.
The only man I'll marry is my darling Valentine.'
In codpiece, wearing breeches, and now named Sebastian.
Julia's hired by Proteus, to be his serving man.

'Fly,' he tells "Sebastian", 'like a bird upon the wing.
To my lady Silvia, with this letter and this ring.'
(Oh Proteus, cruel Proteus, if you but knew the truth.
It's Julia you're speaking to, and not some callow youth)
But as so often happens, things do not go quite as planned.
Both the ring and the letter are rejected out of hand.

Silvia departs Milan with the bold Sir Eglamour,
Arriving in the forest, where went Valentine before.
They're set upon by vagabonds, and overwhelmed by force.
So who will save poor Silvia? Why Proteus of course.
Now, at this point dear reader, please suspend your disbelief.
For Valentine, their prisoner, has now been made their chief.

Proteus, who we now know is nothing but a bounder,
Sidles up to Silvia and puts his arms around her.
'She's yours to do with as you will,' says sneaky Valentine.
(Once more a so-called gentleman has proved to be a swine.)
Thinking her man, Proteus, doesn't love her any more,
Sebastian, aka Julia, falls onto the floor.

The duke and Thurio turn up in midst of all the strife.
When Thurio asks Silvia if she will be his wife.
'Not on your life,' says Valentine, 'lest you're prepared to fight.'
Which puts poor Thurio into a geriatric fright.
The duke's impressed by Valentine and has a change of heart.
He gives him Silvia as wife, till death them both do part.

Proteus then espies the ring worn by his serving man,
As the one he gave Julia when leaving for Milan.
'How came you by this ring?' he asks, 'I gave it Julia.'
'Beneath this male attire,' she says, 'you'll find that I am her.'
She forgives his misdemeanours and awful things he said.
Then swears she'll love him evermore... so be it on her head.

The vagabonds are pardoned, Valentine's restored to grace.
So he and true love, Silvia, can finally embrace.
A double wedding follows in the city of Milan.
But if you were a woman, would you marry either man?

Love's Labour's lost

'This,' says the king, 'is my decree.
I hope that you will all agree
To study and improve your mind,
Whilst keeping clear of womankind.
All women must in future stay,
From court at least a mile away.
It's not that difficult a task.
For just three years, that's all I ask.'

Although Berowne is doubtful still.
Dumaine and Longaville say, 'I will.'
Berowne decides to fall in line,
And signs upon the dotted line.
But then by purest happenstance,
A princess comes from royal France,
On a diplomatic mission,
With a clever proposition.

A plan she hopes will help regain,
The dukedom of old Aquitaine.
The king informs her with a smile.
She must not be within a mile,
Of his palace, especially when
The place is filled with lusty men.

Thus she and her three mates are sent,
To spend the night inside a tent.
When he sees Costard in the park,
Don Armado turns copper's nark.
(Don Armado's a Spanish fool,
Who thinks that he is pretty cool.

Costard's just a poor country lad,
Who it seems has done something bad.)
'Today I saw this naughty thing,
With a woman,' Don tells the king.

The king is not a bit amused,
And tells young Costard: the accused,
'I sentence you from this day on,
To be responsible to Don.
Though Costard likes it not a bit
He'll be in thrall to Don the Twit.

The Don writes out a billet-doux.
Then tells young Costard what to do.
'Take,' he says, 'this little letter
To the lovely Jaquenetta.'
Costard leaves with note in hand.
But things do not go quite as planned.

Along the way he meets Berowne,
Who has a letter of his own.
'Please take,' he says, 'this note of mine.
Deliver it to Rosaline.
The plot is now becoming vexed.
So can you guess what happens next?

Rosaline receives the letter,
That is meant for Jaquenetta.
While Jaquenetta gets the one,
That's written by the young Berowne.
The maid can neither read nor write,
And needs someone who's erudite.

(Step forward please, Holofernes,
And help poor Jaquenetta.
Please read aloud that she may learn,
What's written in the letter.)
Which is of course as is now known.
Not from the Don, but from Berowne.

Not just Berowne, the others too,
Have each composed a billet-doux.
Longaville loves sweet Maria,
And he cannot wait to see her,
Dumaine's in love with Katherine,
The cutest girl he's ever seen.

The king himself is not immune.
He's acting like a lovesick loon.
Though he's forsworn all womankind.
It seems that now he's changed his mind.
And finally he must confess,
His love for France's fair princess.

They hatch a rather silly plan,
Which all agree with to a man.
Each dresses as a Muscovite,
To woo his girl that very night.
And each will swear by stars above,
It's she and no one else he loves.

The girls find out what's going on.
And plan their own deceit anon.
Then to confuse their ardent beaus,
They dress up in each other's clothes.
But finally each one's revealed.
And with a kiss their love is sealed.

A time of merriment ensues.
But then arrives some awful news.
A herald comes to court to say,
The king of France has passed away.
And thus it is with heavy heart,
The princess and her pals depart.

A year and day they'll be away.
Will the lads wait? It's hard to say.
No resolution then it seems.
And no fulfilment of their dreams.

But then, as if to right this wrong,
The play is ended with a song.

A Midsummer Night's Dream

Whilst pondering his wedding to an Amazonian queen,
A courtier comes to ask the Duke if he will intervene,
To stop the budding love affair twixt daughter Hermia,
And Lysander; a man he thinks not good enough for her.

The Duke concurs and tells the girl, 'You must obey your dad.
For if you don't then things for you could turn out very bad.
So wed the man your father's picked, and be a faithful wife.
For if you don't do as he says, you'll surely lose your life.'

But Hermia; a feisty girl, decides to disobey.
Then she and her young lover leave and go far, far away.
He has a wealthy auntie, lives outside Athenian rule.
So that's where they go straight away… this man is no one's fool!

In the forest along the way they meet among the trees,
Helena, with Demetrius, her one and only squeeze.
At this point dear reader - and this can't be overstated,
The details of this story become more complicated.

Helena loves Demetrius, but he does not love her.
The sweet and lovely Hermia's the girl he'd much prefer.
Oberon the King of Fairies, who's in the wood nearby,
Is quarrelling with Titania and here's the reason why.

It's an awkward situation that can't be reconciled.
His queen, the fair Titania, has possession of a child.
A foundling he considers should be his by royal right.
But she refuses to concur... that's why the couple fight.

Meanwhile the ill-matched lovers argue on and on and on.

It's then a brainwave comes unto the mighty Oberon.
'It's time,' he tells his servant, Puck, 'to sort the sorry mess.
By seeking out the woodland flower called Love in Idleness.'

Puck flies off into the wood, but is back within the hour.
Bringing with him magic dust that has a mystic power.
The powder has a potency, unrivalled anywhere,
To turn things once deemed ugly, into something passing fair.

King Oberon tells fairy Puck, 'Go quickly as you can,
And seek throughout the leafy wood until you find a man.
When you find him fast asleep, place this dust into his eyes.
Thus when he wakes he'll fall in love with what he first espies.'

To do his master's bidding, Puck then quickly disappears.
Ere long he comes upon a man dressed in Athenian gear.
Though unaware the man he's found is not the proper one,
He does as he's instructed by the mighty Oberon.

Lysander wakes up from his sleep and swears by stars above,
That Helena, not Hermia's the girl he'll always love.
Elsewhere a motley group of men are practising a play,
To put before the royal duke upon his wedding day.

Just out of sight mischievous Puck hears every word that's said.
And bestows on weaver Bottom a lop-eared ass's head.
The artisans thus filled with fear, run quickly from the scene.
Leaving Bottom all alone with Titania, Fairy Queen.

Who also whilst still fast asleep had dust placed in her eyes,
Thus she when waking from her slumber straight to Bottom flies.
'I love you,' says Titania, 'though you've an ass's head.
My bower's over yonder and it has a double bed.'

In the morning when she's woken,
With the magic spell now broken.
She looks upon the awful sight:
The thing with which she spent the night.
She tells the weaver, 'get thee gone,'

I love not thee, but Oberon.'

Puck takes the ass's head away and Bottom's nightmare ends.
Allowing him to go back home to join his rustic friends.
Meanwhile the lovers quarrel on within the forest deep,
Till tired out by their arguing they all fall fast asleep.

Between them Puck and Oberon decide to put things right.
To end misunderstanding and to ease the lovers' plight,
They gaily sprinkle dust about… they hope will make amends
And see the lovers choose a mate before the story ends.

The magic spell now broken, each one wakes up with a sigh,
And gazes on their partner with a clear and un-drugged eye
Lysander tells sweet Hermia, 'I'll always love you true.'
Demetrius tells Helena, 'I think you're all right too.'

When all the vows of love are done and each has had their say,
They then go back to Athens, to attend the wedding day
Of Hippolyta and Theseus, where they see the show,
Presented by the weaver Bottom, Quince and Flute and Co.

The play the rustic workers have selected to put on,
Is a tale of tragic lovers from ancient Babylon.
That of Pyramus and Thisbe, who as you may recall,
Converse with one another through a hole cut in a wall.

When the play at last is over, and every word's been said.
The players take a grateful bow and then retire to bed.
Hippolyta weds Theseus. Helena weds her beau.
Sweet Hermia weds Lysander, then off the couples go.

A truly happy ending to a most delightful play.
And proof, if proof were needed, love will always find a way.

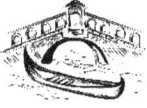

The Merchant of Venice

Our play is set in Venice: where with all his ships at sea,
Antonio the merchant is as sad as he can be.
Bassanio asks the merchant; who for years has been his mate,
To lend him cash so he can take rich Portia on a date.

He'd love to lend his friend the cash, for he's a decent bloke,
Though till his ships all come back home, Antonio's stony broke.
The couple then to Shylock go; a most usurious Jew,
Who lends Antonio all the cash, but then exacts his due.

'Within three months,' he tells him, 'all the debt must be repaid.
If not great retribution on your person will be made.
I'll take a pound of flesh from you, just think how that would feel.
You know my terms Antonio, so do we have a deal?'

And though his friend Bassanio expresses great concern,
Antonio's quite confident his ships will all return.
He takes the money straight away and hands it to his mate.
With cash in hand the merchant's friend can now go on his date.

To Portia's home in Belmont then Bassanio quickly flies.
But on arrival at her house he gets a big surprise.
Before him stand three caskets; each of different metal made.
The proper one when opened gains the hand of this fair maid.

A prince of old Morocco and a prince of Arragon,
Have tried their luck, but came unstuck, now each of them has gone.
A chance then for Bassanio to come in from the cold,
And choose between the caskets made from silver, lead and gold.

Inside the leaden casket by a providence divine,

He finds a note that tells him, I am yours, you lucky swine!
It's joy for him and Portia and his pal Lorenzo too,
Who's run away with Jessica, the daughter of the Jew.

But for the moody merchant things do not go quite so well.
Two ships he owns have foundered in the mighty ocean's swell.
His hefty pile of ducats now reduced to just a few,
How ever will Antonio repay the vengeful Jew?

When Bassanio hears the tidings he tells his blushing bride.
'My pal the merchant's in a fix, I must to Venice ride.
To help poor old Antonio repay the heavy debt.
With money from our coffers Shylock's terms can soon be met.'

But the moneylender's angry, as angry as can be.
And with his knife and scales in hand demands his penalty.
And even though Bassanio offers more than double,
It's not enough to save his friend from his present trouble.

But now the moody merchant gets a really nice surprise,
A lawyer comes to help him out... it's Portia in disguise.
At her side her maid Nerissa, dressed also as a man.
And they are there to carry out a really clever plan.

Portia tells the usurer there's something he should know.
That if he takes a pound of flesh no blood at all must flow.
This crushing revelation strikes the moneylender dumb.
But little does poor Shylock know there's even worse to come.

He's placed in mortal danger a Venetian good and true.
A Christian and a gentleman... an ill-judged thing to do!
Venetian law decrees that when a lethal threat is made,
To the victim and the city, a fine must then be paid.

Full half his wealth must Shylock give unto Antonio.
Straight to the coffers of the state the other half will go.
But there is more bad news to come, as from that very day,
He must adopt the Christian faith and cast his own away.

Poor Shylock's lost his ducats and his daughter's run away.
Worst of all he's now a Christian, he's had a rotten day!
Still unaware the lawyer is his newly wedded wife,
Bassanio pays her with the ring he'd vowed to wear for life.

His band of gold Gratiano gives Nerissa just the same.
Oh how these clever women do enjoy their little game!
They tease their menfolk on and on, till each vows hand on heart,
That with their precious wedding ring they never more will part.

Antonio's ships come safely home, which means he'll earn a pile.
Great cause for celebration and for him to wear a smile.

The Merry Wives of Windsor

This play's about a tubby bloke,
Who's far from home and stony broke.
John Falstaff, a most errant knight,
Who seeks to end his sorry plight,
By wooing to his bachelor bed,
Two girls who are already wed.

To each he sends a billet-doux,
Declaring boldly, *I love you.*
But when the letters they compare,
The ladies soon become aware,
It's just a sneaky little game...
The wording in each one's the same!

Together then they hatch a plan,
To bring to heel this artful man.
'Come visit me,' says Mistress Ford.
'I'd love to welcome you aboard.
I promise you'll enjoy your stay
My husband Frank, is out today.'

But Falstaff's friends, Bardolph and Nym,
Have hatched a plot to scupper him.
They tell Frank Ford, 'while you're away,
Your wife is being led astray,
By Falstaff: a most naughty knight.
How do you mean to put that right?'

To bring the errant knight to book,
Frank dresses up as Mr Brook.
Then in his new identity,

Asks Falstaff while on bended knee,
'Wilt woo for me the mistress Ford?
I so would like to climb aboard.'

'No problem,' says the crafty knight.
'I'm meeting her this very night.'

Mistress Page has a daughter, Anne,
Who's keen as mustard on a man,
Called Fenton: dashing courtier,
Who badly wants to marry her.
But her ma doth much more prefer,
That she should wed a foreigner.

(A wealthy Frenchman, Doctor Caius,
Which by the way's pronounced as Keys.)

Bold Fenton must then first assuage
His girlfriend's mum, the Mistress Page.
To complicate the matter more,
Another's knocking at the door.
Judge Shallow's nephew, Slender named,
Whose ardour simply won't be tamed.

As well as him another two.
What is poor Doctor Caius to do?
A duel of course the only way,
To make the other suitors pay.
But being French his thinking's odd.
He challenges a man of God,
To meet with him and have a fight,
Outside the town that very night.

Dear reader if you're wondering why,
This hapless man's about to die,

Parson Evans is Slender's mate.
And that's why he must meet his fate.
But as in all good comedies,

No one is hurt and no one dies.
An incompetent arranger,
Keeps them both away from danger.
He sends each to a different place,
Which means they don't meet face to face.

And so this little section ends,
With Caius and Evans best of friends.

Meanwhile fat John, the artful knight.
Has Mistress Ford within his sight.
But just as things seem well on track,
The cry goes out,' Her husband's back.'
John's now a very frightened man,
But Ford and Page have got a plan.

They tell him he must get inside,
A laundry basket; there to hide.
Where undetected by her spouse,
He will be taken from the house.
Thereby avoiding any stress,
That might destroy their married bliss.

From thence he's taken on a ride,
To Windsor's smelly riverside.
Where with a most resounding plop,
Poor John is turned out neck and crop.
Amused at Falstaff's grievous pain,
The wives are keen to try again.

Then Mistress Quickly, maid to Caius,
Concocts a plan she's sure will please.
'Without a lie,' she tells fat Jack,
'The Mistress Ford would love you back.
So hie you at the break of day,
To woo her, while Frank Ford's away.'

So off he goes to try once more,
To press the suit that failed before.

But once again comes Mr Brook,
Still hoping to bring John to book.
How then will he this time escape?
The answer... in a woman's cape!

By telling them what went before,
Was just a joke and nothing more,
The women manage to assuage,
The wrath of husbands Ford and Page.
Who, being both fair-minded men,
Agree to trick fat Jack again.

Convinced that he will take the bait,
The Mistress Ford suggests a date,
'At night,' she says, 'when all is dark,
I'll meet with you in Windsor Park.
As Hunter Herne come in disguise.
And you will get a nice surprise.'

When John arrives as Herne arrayed,
A nifty trick on him is played.
Instead of what he most enjoys,
He's hemmed in by a group of boys,
Dressed up as fairies of the night,
Which gives poor John an awful fright.

Meanwhile the lovely daughter Anne,
Slips clean away with her young man.
Which doth her mother much displease.
(She wants her wed to Doctor Caius.)
Anne comes back later; ring on hand...
Not quite what Mistress Ford had planned!

Both Caius and Slender then elope,
Each with a fairy, who they hope,
Is really Anne dressed in disguise.
But to their chagrin and surprise,
Their pursuit brings them little joy,
Inside each costume is a boy!

Instead of looking suave and cool,
John Falstaff's made to look a fool.
Anne's wedding's blessed by mum and dad.
A good laugh then by all is had.
Nobody's hurt. No one is dead.
The play is done... and so to bed.

Much Ado about Nothing

A messenger arrives to say, 'Don Pedro's on his way.'
And that's the opening scene in William Shakespeare's comic play.
Messina's governor, Leonato, opens up his house,
That good Don Pedro and his men may wash and then carouse.

Leonato's very rich and Hero is his daughter.
Young Claudio's a soldier, who's really keen to court her.
But Benedick, his comrade, much prefers the single life.
And swears by all the stars above, he'll never take a wife.

Fair Beatrice, Leonato's niece, a very witty miss,
Declares she too will e'er eschew the state of wedded bliss.
That being wed leaves a girl in something of a pickle.
Men, she tells us all deceive, they're wayward and they're fickle.

Hero and her Claudio decide that they will marry.
But that is seven days away, so awhile they tarry.
They have in mind a strategy: a well deviséd trick,
They hope will bring together Beatrice and Benedick.

First Leonato, Don Pedro and Claudio, groom to be,
Conceal themselves near Benedick, behind a garden tree.
Whilst hid away they plan to talk, and try to make it clear,
That Beatrice adores him, and then hope he'll overhear.

Hero, Ursula and Margaret, have also hatched a plan,
To make quite sure that Beatrice will end up with a man.

They also hide and swear by all the stars that shine above,
They've heard the soldier, Benedick, declare undying love,
For Beatrice: yes, Beatrice, that broiling, bruising miss,

Declaring she's the only girl can bring him wedded bliss.
But there's a man among them on foul disruption bent.
Don John, Don Pedro's brother, a man filled with discontent.
He is a proper rotter and he has a little scheme,
He hopes will bring a sudden ending to young Claudio's dream.

'Go,' he tells Borachio, 'to the bedroom late this night
Of Margaret, Hero's servant, there in full and open sight,
Make love to her, or so pretend, to make it look as though
The one you're making love to is the bride of Claudio.'

On hearing this unwelcome news, poor Claudio's upset.
And jilts bewildered Hero, though the girl's a virgin yet.
'Unjust,' her family members cry, 'she shared nobody's bed.'
Before announcing to the world, 'our lovely daughter's dead.'

It's then the village constable; Dogberry is his name,
Hears how the foul Borachio brought on sweet Hero's shame.
He and his helper Conrad are then locked up in the can.
Which leaves cuckolded Claudio a much embittered man.

Then along comes Leanato and puts his mind at peace.
'Don't worry son,' he tells him, 'you can wed my lovely niece.
She's a little darling and she won't be any trouble.
And it gets much better yet...the girl is Hero's double.'

'Why not?' says twittish Claudio, 'I'm game to have a bash.
As long as she's a cracker and she comes with loads of cash.'
A date is fixed for Claudio, upon a certain day,
To wed the double of his love, who sadly passed away.

But the story told Claudio was just a pack of lies.
And the unsuspecting bridegroom is in for a surprise.
The music plays, the niece arrives and settles at his side.
Young Claudio turns with smiling eyes to gaze upon his bride.

And she, with great decorum, takes the veil from off her head.
Revealing that she's Hero, everybody thought was dead.
The bells ring out; the couple hug, it's time to celebrate.

It's a happy, happy ending and now the pair can mate.
Says Benedick to Beatrice, that broiling, bruising miss.
'So would you care to join with me and live in wedded bliss?'
Much verbal jousting then ensues, but as you've rightly guessed,
The lassie says, 'I do, I do,' both weddings then are blessed.

As You Like It

In his will Sir Rowland de Boys,
Left all he had to both his boys.
But Oliver, the older one,
Feels 't would be a lot more fun,
To distribute his father's wealth,
To no one else, except himself.

Thus, cheated out of his true share,
Orlando now will look elsewhere.
And seek some consolation,
Get a decent education,
And when no longer indigent,
Become the quintessential gent.

Then Charles the wrestler comes to court,
With news of an upsetting sort.
Duke Senior has been banished.
His brother now rules in his stead.
Frederick is his brother's name.
(A man who clearly knows no shame.)

The morrow on a grassy patch,
There will be a wrestling match.
The brave but foolish Orlando,
Decides that he will have a go.
Will Ollie cheer him? Will he heck.
He'd like to see him break his neck.

The day arrives, when in disguise,
Orlando wins: surprise, surprise.
And while the contest's going on,
Fair Rosalind is watching on.

And makes her feelings very plain,
By handing him a lover's chain.

Frederick then, for no good reason,
Charges Rosalind with treason.
With things thus looking very bad,
She leaves to find her dear old dad.
Who à la mode of Robin Hood,
Is hiding in old Arden wood.

Fred's daughter, youthful Celia,
Decides that she'll accompany her.
Thus, hidden from men's' prying eyes,
They leave the court: both in disguise.
In company with Touchstone the clown,
They go to track her father down.

Rosalind's dressed as a mister,
Celia's posing as her sister.
No longer clad in woman's weeds,
Rosalind now is *Ganymede*.
Fair Celia too has done the same,
Aliena now is her name.

Orlando too's a worried man,
And leaves as quickly as he can,
For that same forest, where he'll hide,
With servant, Adam, at his side.
But will the fateful stars align?
And will he meet fair Rosalind?

Along the way they bump into,
A shepherd boy who's feeling blue.
He's just been dealt a bitter blow.
Phebe, his love, has told him, 'no.'
(Poor Silvius, he's dejected.
It's not nice to be rejected)

The shepherd, Corin, then appears.

A man much more advanced in years.
Old Corin is in desperate need.
So sells his farm to *Ganymede*.
(No more a courtly life for her,
A rustic one she'd much prefer.)

The exiled Senior meanwhile,
Is parted from his stately pile,
And now is living happily,
Beneath the leafy greenwood tree,
With huntsmen and a motley crew,
And Jaques, who is always blue.

Orlando, like a lovesick cow,
Hangs odes of love upon the bough.
Which he hopes his love will find.
(I mean, of course, fair Rosalind)
A little later, right on cue,
Fair Rosalind comes into view.

And then; still dressed up as a man,
The lass enacts a cunning plan.
'Pretend,' she says to Orlando,
'I am the girl that you love so.
Woo me as a lover would,
Right here, in leafy Arden Wood.'

Elsewhere a simple lad called Will,
Is swallowing a bitter pill.
Because she's fallen for the clown,
His girlfriend Audrey's turned him down,
Poor William gets the old heave-ho.
As off to Touchstone Audrey goes.

Looking for his younger brother,
Ollie has a spot of bother.
Attacked by beasts along the way,
Orlando comes and saves the day.
It's here the plot gets even more,

More complicated than before.

Sweet Phebe falls for *Ganymede*.
(That's girl on girl, so won't succeed.)
Then Oliver goes gooey-eyed,
And wants Aliena as his bride.
Silvius, who'd been rejected,
This time has his vow accepted.

Rosalind ends her cross-dressing,
And straightway gets her father's blessing,
To wed who long has been her beau,
The fine upstanding Orlando.
Three happy couples, plus one more.
Touchstone and Audrey, that makes four.

We hear that Frederick, Celia's dad;
Has lost the plot and gone quite mad.
He's disappeared from daily sight,
And now lives as an anchorite.
So now it's time to celebrate,
And settle on a wedding date.

Four happy couples all avow,
To wed and live beneath the bough.
Hymen, god of marriage descends.
And that is how the action ends.

All's Well that ends Well

Helena has her eye upon,
Young Bertram Duke of Rossillion.
And though Helena's far from plain,
Young Bertram treats her with disdain.
He will not take her as a mate,
For she is not of high estate.

It's most unfair that he should mock.
Her father was a famous doc.
But he's now dead, sad to report.
So she is now a ward of court.
Looked after by the countess who,
Has lost her loving husband too.

Young Bertram goes from Rossillion.
Sweet, young Helena follows on.
Where at the royal court of France,
They meet by purest happenstance!
It's now we focus on the king,
Who's very ill; the poor old thing.

On seeing that the monarch's ill,
Helena offers him a pill.
It's now a case of make or break.
Helena's life is now at stake.
For if it fails to do the trick,
She'll lose her napper pretty quick.
Eventually she has a go.
But will it cure him; yes or no?

Hip, hip hooray the king is cured.
Helena's future is assured.

So now we have a grateful king,
Who'll grant Helena anything.
Of course her mind is set upon,
Young Bertram from Rossillion.

He greets her offer with a frown.
As once again he turns her down.

The King then speaks and makes it plain,
That Bertram ought to think again.
That straightaway the pair should wed,
And hurry to the wedding bed.
But Bert's unwilling to do this.
(Won't even give the girl a kiss!)

But oh it is a foolish thing,
To argue with an angry king.
And very soon he will find out,
The king has got a lot of clout.
So to appease the angry king,
Young Bertram does the decent thing.

But he has no real intention,
Of complying with convention.
He just ignores the wedding bed,
And hurries off to war instead.
With false Parolles at his side,
He leaves behind his blushing bride.

Bidding Helena fond adieu,
He tells her what she needs to do.
Produce,' he says, 'a child like me,
'While I'm away in Italy,
For only when I've fatherhood,
Will I return and stay for good.'

Thus far she hasn't been defiled.
So how will she produce a child?
The answer is a strategy,

To which a widow holds the key.
She gives the widow cash in hand.
And then a clever ploy is planned.

The widow has a daughter fair,
With whom their little plan they share
Diana is the daughter's name.
And she'll join in their little game.

Because he thinks his wife is dead,
Bert wants to share Diana's bed.
Diana says she'll lie beside
The man who wants her as his bride.
And so a secret tryst's arranged.
At which the sleeping partner's changed.

Instead of Di. between the sheets,
It is in fact his wife he meets.

The upshot of this silly stuff,
Is that Helena's up the duff.
Instead of seeming pretty cool,
Bert is made to look a fool.

Now everything has gone to plan.
At last Helena has her man.

The girl is filled with untold joy.
Anon she'll have a girl or boy.
As Bert's achieved his fatherhood
Things now are looking pretty good.
Parolles, who led Bert astray,
Lives on to fight another day.

And so as far as we can tell,
Things all have ended pretty well.

Troilus and Cressida

Priam has a lot of sons; nearly every one's a boy.
But still somehow has time to be the ruling king of Troy.
Troilus is his youngest son and he loves a Trojan lass.
Her name is Cressida. And she has got a lot of class.

Her uncle, named Pandarus, travels back and forth between,
With messages and billets-doux, then there's a change of scene.
To the tent of Agamemnon, the Grecian number one,
Who's worried by the fact the Trojans have him on the run.

His top men are in disarray: they're fed up and they're bored.
These days they use their tongues to fight, in preference to the sword.
Trojan Aeneas then drops by with an invitation.
'We challenge you,' he says, ' to a single confrontation.

Put up the very best you have and we will do the same.
The one left standing at the end will gain eternal fame.'
The Trojan's best is Hector, it's Achilles for the Greeks.
But he'll not fight for anything... he's been that way for weeks.

Despite his comrades' pleading, he turns down each loud appeal.
(Perhaps he doesn't feel too well, or has a dodgy heel!)
As there's a possibility that he could end up dead,
Ulysses suggests that Ajax fights Hector in his stead.

The Greeks believe there's a way to prevent more blood and gore.
'Give us fair Helen back,' they say, 'and that will end the war.'
Cassandra, Priam's daughter, is a sort of prophetess,
And tells her dad in her opinion he should acquiesce.

'Cry, Trojans, cry,' she shouts out loud, *'lend me ten thousand eyes,'*
(Act 2,1)
Her pleas though fall on stony ground, how ever hard she tries.
Everybody thinks she's crazy; as nutty as a loon.
And anyway, with Helen there, they'll gain a victory soon.

Pandarus, Cressid's uncle, then sets up a rendezvous,
Twixt Cressida and Troilus, so that they can bill and coo.
Each one swears to love the other, forever and a day.
But isn't that what fresh young lovers almost always say?

Though he's a Trojan, Cressid's dad, has left his kith and kin.
And joined up with the Grecian horde, because he thinks they'll win.
Although this act of treachery was something really bad.
He wants his daughter with him... after all he is her dad.

The mighty Agamemnon is happy to concur,
And Antenor, their captive, is exchanged for Cressida.
So Diomedes toddles off to bring her back to Troy.
But there could be a problem... he's a very pretty boy.

They exchange vows of chastity, ere Troilus lets her go.
Unaware that this decision will bring him lots of woe.
She's smitten with Diomedes; she thinks him quite divine.
It seems her vow of chastity might wither on the vine!

Meanwhile the twittish Ajax and brave Hector go to war.
But neither strikes a fatal blow, and so it's called a draw.
Twixt Hector and Achilles then the insults start to fly.
They both agree to meet next day, when one of them will die.

As if to prove, that just like men, women can be fickle.
Helen says to Paris, 'How about some slap and tickle?'
'Okay,' says the son of Priam, 'be with you right away.'
(But when her hubby finds her out, what will he have to say?)

The lovesick Troilus makes his way to where his Cressid lies.
And finds his girl and Diomedes making goo-goo eyes.
The token Troilus gave her; she now blithely gives away.

A foolish thing for which the lass will surely have to pay.

Now Hector puts his armour on, and sharpens up his knife.
Prepared to fight Achilles and to swiftly end his life.
Do not fight,' says mad Cassandra, ' the portents are awry.
If you battle with Achilles, then you will surely die.'

Troilus too has evil thoughts, rolling round inside his head.
A S A P, he'd like to see young Diomedes dead.
Dressed in his suit of armour, Troilus goes to seek him out.
But he's nowhere to be seen, thus his efforts come to nowt.

It's a bad, bad day for Hector, a rotten day all around.
When Achilles and his mates, catch him resting on the ground.
He's left his sword at home, the twit, and so his fate is sealed.
They skewer him with greatest glee and drag him from the field.

So it's one son less at roll call, now Hector's breathed his last.
And every Trojan living thought he couldn't be surpassed.
In discombobulation and in utter disarray,
They go back to their spouses, which is where we end our play.

Measure for Measure

In old Vienna years ago,
There lived a Duke Vincentio.
Who was unable to address,
The city's sin and lawlessness.
In desperation he turns to,
His deputy, named Angelo.
A man made out of sterner stuff,
Who thinks the law's not tough enough.

Once Vincentio has gone,
Alarmed at what is going on,
Hard Angelo makes up his mind,
To be much stricter... more unkind.
He'll tear down brothels: every one.
Bad news for Mistress Overdone.
She runs a bawdy house in town,
And doesn't want it taken down.

Angelo turns his eye upon,
Young Juliet who's six months gone.
('T was Claudio who'd shared a bed,
With Juliet whilst still unwed.)
'A heinous crime,' says Angelo.
So straight off to the jail you go,'

Claudio's sister when she hears,
Breaks down into a flood of tears.
She goes straight to hard Angelo,
And begs him let her brother go.
'I could,' he says, 'let Claudio free,
But only if you'll sleep with me.'

But Isabella's pure as snow.
And answers with a great big, no.
She says,' It simply can't be done.
I'm training to become a nun.'

'So be it then,' says Angelo.
'If that's the case, he'll have to go.
If I can't have my evil way,
Your Claudio will have to pay.'
Which presents a great dilemma,
For the saintly Isabella.
If she declines to share his bed.
Her brother Claudio is dead.

A man dressed as a monk appears,
To calm poor Isabella's fears.
(It's not a monk, as we now know.
It is the duke Vincentio.)
He says he'll help her if he can,
And hatches out a clever plan.
By which her brother will be free,
And she will still a virgin be.

'Go forth,' he says, 'arrange a date,
On which you two will copulate.
But when he climbs into the bed,
His ex will be there in your stead.'
(Mariana was his girlfriend,
But that came to a sudden end.
When he discovered she'd no dough,
He gave the lass the old heave-ho!)

The rendezvous then goes ahead.
The erstwhile couple share a bed.
So will poor Claudio be freed,
Now Angelo has done the deed?
The answer to this question's no.
As double dealing Angelo,
Instructs the axe man, Abhorson,

To go ahead and get it done.
Return' he says, ' with Claudio's head,
As living proof that he is dead.'

Now's the time for Vincentio,
To let the other players know,
That he's their leader in disguise,
And doffs his cloak before their eyes.
'Do not,' he says, 'send Claudio's head.
But send him *Ragozine's instead.'
(*A thief who's died and gone to hell,
Which for our hero works out well!)

The thief's his perfect lookalike.
Now Claudio can take a hike.

He thanks the powers that be above,
And goes back to his lady love.
But Isabella's told he's dead.
And though this news is falsely said,
The would be nun berates the man,
Who said, 'I'll free him if I can.'
She's then advised to ask the duke,
If he will give a strong rebuke,
To Angelo for being bad,
And acting like a proper cad.

Dressed up in all his finery,
The Duke returns to hear her plea.
However, he's a rum old bird,
And when her earnest plea is heard,
He shakes his head and says,' nay, nay.
I don't believe a word you say.'

Why does he tease the poor girl so?
The audience will want to know.
He then reveals he played a trick,
By posing as Friar Ludowick.

And then shows great compassion to,
Both Angelo and Claudio.

The former and his ex are wed.
(They had to as they'd shared a bed!)
Fair Juliet and Claudio too,
Their wedding vows can now renew.
The Duke then asks the nun to be,
'How would you like to marry me?'

A good result for everyone.
And now our play is nearly done.
Except that punkish Keepdown Kate,
Is told to fix a wedding date
With Lucio, young Claudio's friend,
Who then comes to a grisly end.
Soon after Lucio is wed,
The duke decrees, off with his head.

A speedy and a stern rebuke,
For slagging off the high-born duke!

'What's mine is yours, and what is yours is mine,' (Act V, 1)
Is practically the closing line.
It's spoken by Vincentio.
But does she answer yes or no?
Will Shakespeare doesn't care to say.
And that's the finish of the play.

Twelfth Night

In old Illyria lives a lord, who has one aim in life.
To take the fair Olivia to be his wedded wife.
But Olivia is grieving and does not want to know.
That's why the lord Orsino's such a moody so and so.
'Oh me, oh my,' you'll hear him cry, from morning until night.
With tear-stained eyes and runny nose he looks an awful sight.

But while the lord is weeping, there's lightning and there's thunder.
And in the twinkling of an eye a ship has gone under.
A highborn woman named Viola makes it to the shore,
But fears her twin, Sebastian, is on the ocean floor.
Alone, alone and all alone in a strange land stranded.
She hasn't got a satnav and knows not where she's landed.

In trousers, boots and jerkin clad, Viola leaves the shore.
And goes to where Orsino lives and knocks upon his door.
Viola; now named Cesario, and dressed like a man.
Asks Orsino, 'Can you use me?' Orsino says, 'I can.'
She's very soon promoted to the higher rank of page.
For which the gloomy, doomy lord pays her a living wage.

Viola as Cesario, then starts to carry notes,
Unto the sad Olivia, on whom the lord still dotes.
Cesario brings a twinkle to the sad Olivia's eye.
It's here that things begin to go a little bit awry.

Viola loves Orsino, but while dressed in male attire,
She cannot tell the moody lord that he's her heart's desire.
Olivia loves Cesario; she thinks he's rather sweet.
And thus the three-way love affair is more or less complete.

Away from these liaisons and affairs that touch the heart.
There are many others who will play a vital part.
Olivia's uncle, Toby Belch, a boozer nonpareil;
His friend Sir Andrew Augicheek, who gives his niece the eye;
A clever clown named Feste and Maria who's the maid;
The head of house Malvolio, who's humourless and staid.

The pretty maid Maria has a clever little plan,
To mortify Malvolio, who is a hated man.
Pretending she's Olivia she writes a billet doux.
Declaring in the strongest terms... I am in love with you.
Smile a lot, the letter says, and be a happy fellow.
Most of all wear garters and make sure they're coloured yellow.

Sebastian; Viola's brother, who she thought had drowned,
Arrives with friend Antonio, then heads straight to the town.
Olivia 's so much better now; in fact, she's feeling grand.
And wants to ask Cesario if he will give his hand.
She means of course not just his hand, but each and every part.
Her grieving done she's now prepared to give away her heart.

The jealous Andrew Augicheek: a drunkard and a fool,
Hates the bold Cesario and suggests the two should duel.
But when it's time to fight the duel, Sebastian appears.
Sir Toby joins in, thus we know it's bound to end in tears.

In the midst of much confusion, Olivia arrives.
'Put up your swords,' she tells them, thus saving both their lives.
Thinking he's Cesario, she asks Sebastian for his hand.
Sebastian agrees to wed, but cannot understand,
Why a gal he's never met, is so keen to tie the knot.
It's yet another whacky twist in this confusing plot.

When Sebastian's friend, Antonio, is thrown into jail.
He turns to his old mate to ask if he'll put up the bail.
Antonio and Orsino are not good friends you see.
(Orsino's not forgiven him for piracy at sea.)
But disappointment follows, when his erstwhile pal says no.
Though as we know it's not his friend, but twin Cesario.

Meantime the poor Malvolio is locked up in a cell.
Where Toby and Maria make his life a living hell.
Feste agrees to visits him, while as a cleric clad.
And with the greatest gravity, declares him to be mad.

Malvolio, poor chap, is well and truly in the cart.
Till Sir Toby and the rest have a sudden change of heart.
They put their heads together and decide 't would be better.
If Malvolio should send Olivia a letter.

Sebastian finds his twin still lives, thus both are filled with joy.
Orsino weds Viola, now he knows she's not a boy.
Sir Toby weds Maria. Antonio's forgiven.
And reunited with his pal, when released from prison.
The air is filled with joyous laughter; things have turned out well.
Except for poor Malvolio, who's still as mad as hell.

Feste takes up his lute and sings, '*it raineth every day.*' (*Act V, 1*)

And on this happy note we reach the end of this great play.

The Tragedies

Titus Andronicus

His sons once numbered twenty-five,
But now remain just four alive.
The others all in battles fought.
That's why their lives were very short.

But Titus has found recompense,
In bringing those who caused offence,
Back to the capital in chains,
As some reward for all his pains.

With his captive, Aaron the Moor;
The queen of Goths and many more,
The vengeful Titus comes back home
Unto the family tomb in Rome.

He's there to bury his dead son:
His dead son number twenty-one.

His captive the queen Tamora,
Has three sons who all adore her.
There's Chiron and there's Alarbus,
And one more called Demitrius.

To gain revenge Andronicus,
Bumps off the one called Alarbus.
Which makes his brothers pretty sad.
And queen Tamora hopping mad.

But then the strangest twist of fate.
The emperor wants her for his mate.
But Tamora, the blushing bride,

Is far from being satisfied.

Though being married seems like fun.
She'd rather have two men than one.
So with the Moor, her fancy man,
She hatches out a cunning plan.

'There's work,' she tells him, 'to be done.
To shame the man who killed my son.'
He's told to slay Bassanius,
The brother of Saturninus.

The two sons of Andronicus:
Young Quintus and young Martius
Are blamed. And though there's nothing proved.
Both brothers have their heads removed.

But even though his sons have died,
The queen is still not satisfied.
And puts another plot in train,
To bring mad Titus yet more pain.

She tells her sons, 'rape his daughter.
Do it well and give no quarter.'
They do the deed as ma commands.
They rape her then cut off her hands.

The poor girl's tongue is ripped out too.
(A most unpleasant thing to do).
No hands to point, no tongue to tell,
Lavinia's life's a living hell.

But Titus has a clever trick.
He gives Lavinia a stick.
Though,' he says, ' you haven't a hand.
Put stick in 't mouth, and write in 't sand,
The names of those who did this deed.'
She writes it down, so he can read.

Their guilt now proved beyond a doubt,
He plans to wipe the culprits out.
His last son's then kicked out of Rome.
Now Titus is alone at home.

His hair's now turned the colour grey.
He's looking madder by the day.
But this is just a crafty ruse,
Designed to fuddle and confuse.

For what he really has in mind,
Is dinner of a different kind.
For soon Tamora's sons will die.
Then be served to her in a pie.

Then when the grisly dinner's done,
He slays Tamora just for fun.
Followed by the further slaughter,
Of Lavinia - his own daughter.

What great fun thinks Saturninus,
Who ere he's killed by Lucius,
Gets rid of the eponymous,
Completely mad Andronicus.

Things now go into overdrive.
Aaron the Moor's interred alive.
Tamora, who's just popped her clogs,
Is eaten by a pack of dogs.

So who is left among this shower,
To take hold on the reins of power?
Who else but master Lucius,
Son of the late Andronicus.

Romeo and Juliet

And now it's time that you should know,
The story of young Romeo.
A tale of love from years gone by,
That yet brings tears into the eye.

To start with here's a vital clue.
Romeo is a Montague.
The girl he wants is Juliet,
Who sadly is a Capulet.
Which leaves them in an awful fix.
Like oil and water, they don't mix.

At the moment Romeo's sad.
The girlfriend situation's bad.
He's just been told by Rosaline,
'Forget it mate, I'll ne'er be thine.'

It's then he takes an awful chance,
By going to a family dance,
At the abode of Capulet,
Where he espies fair Juliet.
But there's danger for our hero.
If he's discovered, he'll be zero.

A little kiss and then he leaves.
But hangs about beneath the eaves,
Till Juliet appears above,
To tell the world that she's in love.
When daddy Capulet finds out.
He stamps his foot and hollers out.
'A Montague is not for you.
You need a man whose blood is blue.'

He tells her he is much inclined,
To Paris, who is more refined.

Our Romeo then does a bunk,
And goes to see the local monk.

'Are you willing,' he asks the friar,
'To wed me to my heart's desire?'

The friar agrees immediately.
He thinks the wedding possibly,
Could bring two clans so long at war,
To live in peace for evermore.
So in the morning sharp at nine,
The pair sign on the dotted line.

But trouble's brewing in the street.
As Benvolio and Mercutio meet,
With Tybalt, who's a Capulet,
And cousin to fair Juliet.
A fracas follows straight away,
As deadly swords come into to play.

But ere they've even struck a blow,
Along comes new-wed Romeo.
'I hate you,' Tybalt cries out loud.
'Prepare to be wrapped in a shroud.'
But Romeo declines to fight.
He thinks it simply can't be right,
To quarrel with a person who,
He finds himself related to.

But not so with Mercutio,
He'd like to strike the fatal blow.
He draws his sword and with him fights,
But Tybalt soon puts out his lights.
A most foolhardy thing to do,

As Romeo then runs him through.
Verona's prince is not amused,
To see the law so much abused.
He tells offending Romeo,
'I think it's time for you to go.'

(Poor Romeo is banishéd,
And not yet shared the wedding bed!)

A situation he puts right,
By sleeping with his bride that night.
The morrow morn he parts from her,
Then legs it to old Mantua.

But should she stick with Romeo,
The man who laid her cousin low?
She does, as you'd anticipate,
Decide to share her lover's fate.

The father of young Juliet;
The aforementioned Capulet,
Is unaware his daughter's wed,
To he who struck poor Tybalt dead.

And now he wants her married off,
To Paris, the aforementioned toff.
'What should I do?' she asks her nurse.
'Seems things have gone from bad to worse.'

The answer deals a bitter blow.
'Get rid, ' she says, 'of Romeo
Go tell the world your hubby's dead,
Then wed the gentleman instead.'

Thus, with the situation dire,
She hurries off to see the friar.
Who comes up with an action plan,
For her to be with her old man.
'Drink all,' he says, 'that's in this phial,

'T will knock you out for quite a while.
In fact, for more than just a day.
And make it seem you've passed away.'

While Juliet sleeps the night away,
Old Friar John gets under way,
To Mantua and Romeo,
To tell him all he needs to know.
But by an awful twist of fate,
The friar's delayed and turns up late.

(A mission that was bound to fail.
He should have used the Royal Mail!)
From Balthasar he gets instead,
The crushing news that Juliet's dead.

A potent drug in his pocket,
Romeo leaves like a rocket,
To be with Juliet, his wife.
Once there he too will end his life.

While on his way to Juliet's tomb,
He meets with Paris; would be groom.
And there beneath the cloak of night,
They draw their swords and start to fight.

With Paris dead upon the ground,
Our hero quickly turns around.
Then as directed by the script,
Heads straight off to the family crypt.

Where lies his sweetheart in a gown,
Her chest not going up or down.
'She's dead,' the poor lad loudly cries.
Then drinks the potion down and dies.

The meddlesome friar then appears.
Juliet wakes and through her tears,
Espies the man she's fallen for,

Dead in a heap upon the floor.

Unhappy scene, unhappy wife.
She reaches down and takes his knife.
The girl's now feeling very stressed,
And sinks the knife deep in her chest.

The families swear from that day hence,
They'll speak no word to cause offence.
To live in peace and make amends.
And that is where the story ends.

Julius Caesar

Amid the hurly-burly of the Feast of Lupercal,
Julius is joined by Antony, who long has been his pal.
'Take this,' he says to Julius, offering him the crown.
But Julius, feigning modesty, three times turns it down.

His coyness cuts no ice at all with those who know him well.
For all his triumphs in the field have caused his head to swell.
As Caesar leaves the Lupercal a warning voice is heard.
'Beware the Ides of March,' it cries, which Caesar thinks absurd. (*Act
I, scene 2)*

But unbeknown to Caesar, there's much plotting going on.
Casca, Cinna and Ligarius want to see him gone.
As do Flavius and Cimber and Marcus Brutus too.
So they convene a meeting, to decide what they should do.

Caesar's wife, Calphurnia, has a horrid dream that night.
She dreams her husband will be killed, which gives her quite a
fright.
Her pleas for him to stay at home are wasted on the air.
As to the Senate he repairs, completely unaware
That the plotters have decided it's time for him to go.
Each one has brought a knife along and each will strike a blow.

They gather round him in a ring.
And each takes out his pointy thing.
Then sticks it in their evil boss,
Which makes him very, very cross.

'Et tu Brute,' (*Act 3,1*) great Caesar cries.
And then the poor old codger dies.

On hearing Caesar is no more,
Antony, Brutus doth implore...
'Oh please,' he says, 'let it be me,
That gives the funeral oratory.'

But Brutus is a clever chap and hopes that he can sway,
The people gathered and explain great Caesar's death away.
'He was ambitious to a fault,' he tells the swelling throng.
'That's why we had to bump him off. So how can that be wrong?'

So now it's time for Antony to say a word or two,
He asks the crowd to lend their ears, which they all gladly do.
He tells them that dear Brutus is an honest man withal.
And with this oft repeated phrase he holds the crowd in thrall.

But Romans are a knowing lot, and see the irony.
They realise this speech is more than simple eulogy.
That Brutus and his motley crew are nothing but a shower:
A bunch of nasty egotists intent on gaining power.

Thus, knowing that the game is up, that they have been undone.
It's time for Brutus and the rest to shut up shop and run.
Mark Antony, Octavius and Lepidus as well,
Pursue the plotters all the way, like bats from out of Hell;
From Rome through rural Italy, beneath a clear blue sky.
To Sardis by the rugged plain of ancient Philippi.

Mark Antony, Octavius and Lepidus prepare,
To fight with Caesar's killers and thus end the whole affair.
Cassius and Marcus Brutus then argue on and on,
About the way to fight the fight until the day is won.
'Attack,' says Marcus Brutus, but friend Cassius says him nay.
'Just let them come to us,' he says, 'that's how we'll win the day.'

But Brutus wins the argument. The battle lines are drawn.
The deadly foes will meet for sure upon the morrow morn.
Upon the eve of battle there's an uninvited guest.
(The ghost of murdered Caesar, in a bloodstained toga dressed.)

'I shall see thee at Philippi,'(Act 4, Scene3) ◀ the ghostly form intones.
'Buzz off,' says Marcus Brutus, 'I must rest my weary bones.'

And so the fateful day arrives; a day for men to die.
But who will take the honours on the plain of Philippi?
At first the battle goes along exactly as they'd planned.
It seems that Brutus and his mates have gained the upper hand.
Strangely thinking all is lost, that it's time for him to go,
Cassius bids the world farewell, then strikes the fatal blow.

For Marcus Brutus things look grim.
So what now will become of him?
With Cassius gone what chance has he,
To win the final victory?
Depressed, alone and feeling blue,
There's only one thing left to do.
To die the way each Roman knows...
Out comes the sword and in it goes.

Caesar's murder has been avenged; his killers all are dead.
His adopted son Octavius, will rule in his stead.
When Antony surveys the scene, a tear comes to his eye.
Then he's told the corpse of Brutus, lies in the field nearby.

'He was,' says Marcus Antony, 'the noblest of them all.'
And with this final utterance the curtain now can fall.

Hamlet

On the battlements of Elsinore in the depths of darkest night.
Horatio and two watchmen, all get an awful fright.
The ghost of Hamlet's father, who popped off the other day,
Appears before their very eyes, then quickly fades away.

Naughty Claudius, his brother, helped by the late king's wife,
Conspired together in a plot to take the poor chap's life.
Whilst the king was taking forty winks, Claudius came near.
And poured a vial of poison in his unsuspecting ear.

The ghost explains to Hamlet how the dirty deed was done.
And says, 'Yu must avenge my death. Go bump him off my son.'
But Hamlet's a gentle soul, given to contemplation.
How then should he go about an assassination?

These are troublous times for Hamlet; his mum now shares a bed,
With Claudius his uncle, who his late dad now wants dead.
His behaviour's rather odd. He's been shaken to the core.
He even tells his girlfriend, 'I don't love you anymore.'

But Claudius and Gertrude, (let us call them Gert and Claud),
Have seen a change in Hamlet that cannot be ignored.
Rosencrantz and Guildenstern, Hamlet's friends since yesteryear,
Are told to watch and find out why he's acting rather queer.

'It must be,' says Polonius, 'that Hamlet's much beguiled,
By my girl Ophelia: she'd drive any fellow wild.'

A group of travelling actors then arrives in Elsinore.
But Hamlet has a word with them before they take the floor.
He tells them to make changes, which he hopes will demonstrate,

That now a killer occupies the Danish seat of state.

In the play within the play a murder is depicted.
At this point King Claud leaps up, looking sore afflicted.
Just like a scalded cat he flees with all the speed he's got.
It seems Prince Hamlet's little ploy has really hit the spot!

It's proof, if proof were needed, he's a bounder and a cad.
That he's the one who did the deed that killed his dear old dad.
And though against his gentle nature, kill the king he must.
So at some point the evil Claud is bound to bite the dust.

To kill or not to kill the king, that's the burning question.
There's no point in hoping he will die from indigestion.
But it's essential to the plot the king should stay alive.
For he has many lines to speak, in acts three, four and five.

When Hamlet goes as bidden, to the bedroom of his mum,
He tells her what he thinks of her, how rotten she's become.
Believing that her son intends to deal a fatal blow,
The queen declares in future she'll be pure as driven snow

In the midst of this kerfuffle, from the arras that's nearby,
Polonius, who is hidden there, lets out a muffled cry.
Hamlet thinks it must be Claud, although he can't be certain.
And takes his sword from out its sheath, then stabs him through the
curtain

The end of Lord Polonius with two more acts to go.
And now the ghost of Hamlet's dad puts in another show.
It's just a flying visit, to remind his moody son,
He's promised that he'll kill the king, which he has not yet done.

Gert asks with consternation, for the ghost she cannot see.
'How is't with you that you do bend your eye on vacancy?' *(Act 3, 4)*

She thinks her son is going mad, or does he just pretend?
The answer we'll discover ere the play is at an end.
Hamlet sails disconsolate, to the place where he's been banned.

To meet the King of England, in that green and pleasant land,
Rosencrantz and Guildenstern have also climbed aboard.
They have a sealed-up letter, written by that rotter Claud.

The letter has but one request, that's clear as clear can be.
'Would you please,' it asks the king, 'bump Prince Hamlet off for me?'

Meanwhile Ophelia, struck with grief, is slowly going mad.
Her lover's left, she's bereft and she's lost her dear old dad.
The fates are all against her; it's the end of loves young dream.
So she decides to end it all by drowning in a stream.

Discovering what has happened to his sister and his dad,
Back to Denmark comes Laertes, and he is hopping mad.
The evil Claud takes him aside and whispers in his ear.
'T was Hamlet did them in,' he says, 'to all that's very clear.'

While they are hatching out a plan designed to seal his fate.
Prince Hamlet's at the graveyard with Horatio, his mate.
Having freed himself from pirates, who captured him at sea,
We find Prince Hamlet by the grave, down on his bended knee.
It's then he sees a skull that lies upon the sullen earth.
That once belonged to Yorick, a man of infinite mirth.

As the coffin with Ophelia in it comes on to the stage,
Her brother, Lord Laertes, flies into a burning rage.
He and Hamlet argue over which one loved her best.
It's only when they're torn apart, Ophelia's laid to rest.

With the funeral service over, it's back then to the court.
Where Hamlet's asked if he'd enjoy a little bit of sport.
A man named Osric tells him that it's just a bit of fun.
Where he and Lord Laertes face each other one to one.

It's a plot concocted by the evil, scheming Claud.
That unbeknown to Hamlet, includes a poisoned sword.
All it will take to kill him is the merest little scratch.
Which will give the Lord Laertes the game, the set and match.

It's Hamlet gets the first strike in, and wounds him in the arm.
But the weapon's free of poison, and does him little harm.
In the brouhaha that follows, the swords fall to the ground.
As unbeknown to either man, the two get switched around.

'Well done,' says Claud and offers up a goblet filled with wine.
'I'm a bit tied up,' says Hamlet, 'I therefore must decline.'
But Gert is not so reticent: she takes it from the king.
And in the blinking of an eye she dies, the poor old thing.

Laertes, now envenomed by the sword in Hamlet's hand,
Is on the way to paradise, which wasn't what was planned.
Ere he dies the lad admits his everlasting shame.
'I can no more,' he tells the prince, *'the king, the king's to blame.'*

(Act 5,2)
So Hamlet does the decent thing, he runs the rotter through.
As if that's not enough, he makes him drink the wine down too!
Both Claud and Gert; Laertes too, have bid the world goodbye.
We're almost at the point where wounded Hamlet too must die.

Before he goes he calls his pal, Horatio to his side.
'Tell the world,' he bids him, 'exactly how and why I died.'
When Prince Fortinbras of Norway arrives in Elsinore,
He sees four blooded bodies, lying there upon the floor.

The play's almost over, there's little more that needs be said.
Except to tell you Rosencrantz and Guildenstern are dead.
Four soldiers lift up Hamlet's corpse and carry it away.
And now the curtain falls on William Shakespeare's longest play.

Othello, the Moor of Venice

In Venice there's a Moorish man; Othello is his name.
A general who has served his land and gained a lot of fame.
He needs a new lieutenant but who should he promote?
After much consideration, young Cassio gets the vote.

When the news gets to Iago he flies into a tizz.
The job that's gone to Cassio should really have been his.
And though for poor Iago it has been a shocking day,
He smiles, but through his smile avows to make Othello pay.

By using innuendo, he is hoping by degrees,
To bring the objects of his malice crashing to their knees.
Desdemona, Othello's wife, is where he will begin.
By crafty ruse and subterfuge, he'll try to rope her in.

Othello then is posted to a far and distant isle.
Where Desdemona joins him after just a little while.
Iago and his wife Emelia also come along.
Once there Iago wastes no time in making things go wrong.

He starts by getting Cassio as drunk as he can be.
Then calls on Roderigo; for at one time it was he,
Who sometime in the recent past was Desdemona's beau.
And even though she's married now, he'd like another go

Iago tells Roderigo, Desdemona has a yen,
To see him and for them to be an item once again.
Drunk as a skunk young Cassio then stumbles into sight.
Then he and Roderigo get into a bruising fight.

A very, very silly thing for Cassio to do.

It's something that in days to come he'll have good cause to rue.
Drunken Cassio's arrested and flung into the clink.
Where he's fed on bread and water, and has much time to think.

But when his boss Othello hears that he's been in a fray,
His status as an officer will finish straight away.
But this is just the start of things, Iago's more in store.
He tells the hapless Cassio, 'go knock on Desi's door.

Fall down onto your bended knee and with the lady plead.
For she and she alone can help you in your hour of need.'
Then dirty dog Iago leads Othello to the place,
Where young Cassio and Desi are standing face to face.

The sight of them together fills Othello with despair.
He wrongly thinks his lovely wife is having an affair.
And then by fair Emilia, a handkerchief is found,
Where, by the purest happenstance, it fell down the ground.

The kerchief is a gift Othello gave unto his wife.
Which proves to be the catalyst for much ensuing strife.
Iago takes the handkerchief and plants it by the bed
Of Cassio, who gives it to a woman who's unwed.
A woman named Bianca, who's a lady of the night.
Desdemona and Othello then get into a fight.

He wants to know why Cassio is in possession of
The handkerchief he gave her, as a token of his love.
And though she says she's innocent he simply will not hear,
Which means the end for Cassio is drawing ever near.

Othello tells Roderigo that Cassio must die.
Then with Iago at his side to Cassio's home they fly.
But Roderigo's not that good at doing people in.
Instead of bumping Cassio off, he stabs him in the shin

Cassio is unaware 't was Iago and not he,
Who stabbed the young Roderigo, somewhere below the knee.
It's a problem for Othello and for Iago too.

So the dirty rotten plotter does what he has to do.
This time his aim is better and with one unerring stab,
He makes sure Roderigo doesn't get the chance to blab.
Though blameless of the awful crime, heaped upon her head,
Othello kills poor Desdemona, lying in her bed.

Iago's wife Emilia then enters in the fray,
And shocks the socks off everyone with what she has to say.
Now realising that her man is nothing but a cad.
She tries her best to make it clear why things have turned out bad.

Emelia tells the truth of how the handkerchief was found.
How unbeknown to Desdemona it fell to the ground.
But ere she can elaborate Iago strikes her down.
Then leaves his dying wife behind and legs it out of town.

Still claiming to be innocent he's caught and thrown in jail.
But letters found on Roderigo tell a different tale.
You might expect Othello to strike Iago dead.
But filled with loathing and remorse, he kills himself instead.

The sad Tale of King Lear

Lear was an early British king,
Who loved his girls like anything.
This crafty man devised a test,
To find out which one loved him best.

The eldest pair; two slimy toads,
Say, 'Daddy dear we love you loads.'
The third and youngest will not say,
And so he sends her on her way.

'Be it,' he says, 'upon your head.
You'll get no dosh when I am dead.
Both Regan and good Goneril
Shall share the proceeds of the will.'

'Don't care,' says young Cordelia fair.
Those two old crows can have my share.'
Then leaves them all without a glance,
And goes to wed the King of France.

Then Goneril and her sibling,
Set out to undermine the king.
A shocking way to treat their dad,
And that's why poor old Lear goes mad.

That night the king puts in his teeth
And sets out for the nearest heath.
Wrapped in a shawl of purest wool,
Accompanied by the royal fool.

Then Edmund, Gloucester's bastard son,

Decides he'll have a bit of fun,
And tells old Gloucester with a grin
'Your Edgar wants to do you in.'

'No not my Edgar,' Gloucester cries;
Not knowing it's a pack of lies.
Then scared and stunned with disbelief,
Poor Edgar too heads for the heath.

Thinking it better for a while,
To leave behind his stately pile
He disappears fast as he can,
Disguised as Tom, a beggar man.

Old Lear, now feeling desolate,
Is pleased when Gloucester, his old mate,
Decides he'll do all that he can,
To help the poor unhappy man.

Then to the stage comes Goneril,
To put a spoke in Gloucester's wheel.
She takes the noble by surprise,
And gouges out the poor chap's eyes.

'My eyes are gone I cannot see,'
The old man cries out plaintively.
And thus goes blindly wandering,
Without a map or anything.

Later on this hapless rover,
Comes upon a town called Dover.
Whereat by happenstance most queer,
He bumps into his old friend Lear.

Cordelia comes with Gallic host,
To save the dad she loves the most.
But when the fearsome Brits appear,
The Frenchmen flee in mortal fear.

Cordelia's captured by the Brits,
And cut up into little bits.
Things then go quickly to the dogs,
As poor old Gloucester pops his clogs.

In order not to disappoint,
There's rumpy-pumpy at this point.
When evil Edmund has his will,
With Regan and with Goneril.

Then bad and nasty Goneril,
Decides to go in for the kill.
And poisons Regan out of spite,
Then tops herself to put things right.

News of his youngest daughter's death,
Leaves poor old King Lear quite bereft.
And now with all his daughters gone,
He breathes his last and passes on.

With Lear and all his family dead,
The country's left without a head.
So Albany, Edgar and Kent,
All join to form a government.

When William Shakespeare wrote this play.
He must have had a bad hair day.
A stirring tale most would agree.
But lacking in frivolity.

Macbeth

The play begins with witches three upon the blasted moor.
They greet Macbeth and Banquo, who have just returned from war.
'Anon,' the witches tell Macbeth, 'you'll King of Scotland be.
And your old mucker Banquo will beget a dynasty.'

The witches also prophesy Macbeth will be a Thane.
Then he and Banquo leave the moor and head off down the lane.
Macbeth then sends a letter to his current home address:
A cold and draughty castle by the banks of River Ness.

When his wife receives the letter, she goes into a spin.
And plots a course of slaughter that'll make her hubby king.
She tells him, 'Murder Duncan, for it's only when he's dead,
That you can sit upon the throne, the crown upon your head.'

Though he protests with vehemence, his evil wife wins out.
And finally Macbeth agrees, though riddled through with doubt.
He creeps into the chamber, where King Duncan is abed.
And stabs him with a dagger, till he's absolutely dead.

Macbeth then leaves the chamber to rejoin his scheming wife,
Who throws a wobbly when she sees he still has got the knife.
She takes it quickly from him and returns to Duncan's door.
Then lays it by two drunken servants, prostrate on the floor.

Though guiltless these two fellows have the blame heaped on their head.
Then straight away Macbeth steps in and strikes the couple dead.
Knowing that to hang around will lead to certain death.
Both Duncan's sons put miles between themselves and mad Macbeth,

Now that he's king he concentrates on Banquo, his old mate.
And plots a way to bring his friend unto an early fate.
He hires a gang of murderers to carry out the deed…
A simple task in which they only partially succeed.

They manage to kill Banquo, though they fail to slay his son.
Who flees the scene and disappears into the setting sun.
Macbeth ordains a royal feast to entertain his peers.
And even though he's not invited, Banquo's ghost appears.

The sight of his old mucker floating high above his head,
Turns Macbeth into a jelly and fills him up with dread.
And though his pushy missus tries her best to calm him down.
It's clear her man's not really fit to wear the royal crown.

In need of lots of TLC, Macbeth returns once more,
To parley with the witches, he first met upon the moor.
'Don't worry dear,' they tell him, 'for no harm to you will come.
The only man can kill you is a man who had no mum.'

Three people dead already and as if that's not enough,
Macbeth then turns his thoughts towards the meddlesome Macduff.
His henchmen go to kill him, but discover he's not there.
And so they slay his wife and kids, which seems a bit unfair.

Weighed down with guilt at what she's done, Macbeth's egregious
wife,
Departs the stage to find a spot to end her sorry life.
Upset by what Macbeth has done, Macduff and Malcolm meet,
To raise a force, they hope will bring the dastard to defeat.

They march away to Birnam Wood, then on to Dunsinane.
It's there Macduff beheads the man who's caused him so much pain.
So now it's time to celebrate: to shout aloud with joy.
And time to say good riddance to a very naughty boy.

Antony and Cleopatra

Sent out to rule in Egypt by his bosses based in Rome,
The triumvir Mark Antony is far away from home.
And though for many, many years to Fulvia he's been wed,
With Cleopatra, Egypt's Queen, he also shares a bed.

But then he gets a letter saying Fulvia is no more.
And a malcontent named Pompey is itching for a war.
It's an order from the Senate that cannot be denied.
So off to Rome he toddles, to be at his boss's side,

In Rome another triumvir, Octavius by name,
Thinks things are bad in Egypt and that Antony's to blame.
Octavius has a sister, her name's Octavia.
To pacify the grumpy man our hero marries her.

It's just a gesture of goodwill; Octavia's rather plain.
It's the gorgeous Cleopatra he longs to see again.

Antony hates Octavius, Octavius hates him.
The chances of them getting on are really rather slim.
It comes therefore as no surprise; we've seen it all before.
Octavius and Antony are very soon at war.

His wife, the plain Octavia, attempts to come between.
But as she tries to make the peace, her spouse departs the scene
He legs it back to Egypt, where he's greeted with a smile,
By the lovely Cleopatra beside the flowing Nile.

Octavius, now Caesar, throws a wobbly when he hears,
And finds it nigh impossible to stop his sister's tears.

He considers it a travesty far beyond belief.
And aims to give our Antony a fair amount of grief.

Though Antony is told it's best to fight him on the land,
By Enobarbus and the rest, who stand at his right hand.
He opts to fight Octavius Caesar on the ocean blue.
It's a really bad decision - and one that he will rue.

('T was Cleo who told Antony to fight upon the land.
Though he's a Roman triumvir, he's putty in her hands.)

Together Cleopatra and her lover then set sail,
To Actium in western Greece, but they are doomed to fail.
When Caesar and his generals start to gain the upper hand,
It soon becomes apparent things have not gone quite as planned.

Cleo soon discovers fighting isn't that much fun.
And with Antony behind her sails off into the sun.
For fleeing from the battle like a pair of frightened mice,
The cowardly pair eventually will pay an awful price.

Still haunted by his failure and the bitterness of loss,
Antony goes to Caesar; the man who's still his boss.
'Forget about the past,' he says, 'that caused us so much pain.
We once were bosom buddies and we could be once again.'

But Caesar will have none of it, he wants to come between
The triumvir he hates so much and his Egyptian queen.
He goes to Cleopatra and he puts her to the test.
'Unless you kill your man,' he says, 'for you there'll be no rest.

For once your lover's been bumped off, just you and you alone,
Will rule in splendid majesty and sit upon the throne.'
But Cleopatra tells him that she never would agree,
To kill the man who's always been her little chickadee.

And so it's off to war again, to battle hand to hand,
Against the mighty Caesar, but this time they fight on land.
At first things go extremely well, our hero wins the day.

But when the fight's resumed next morn his soldiers run away.
The battle well and truly lost our Tony has no doubt
His little treasure, Cleopatra, must have sold him out.

Poor Cleo, fearing for her life, heads to the family tomb,
And everyone assumes the girl has met an early doom.
Believing that his lover's dead; the girl he so adored,
Our Tony does the Roman thing; he falls on to his sword.

He lives for just a little while: just long enough in fact,
To say goodbye to Cleo in the tragic fourteenth act.
When Caesar hears the sorry news about his former friend,
He tells Queen Cleopatra he will try to make amends.

'You must come back with me,' he says, 'to sunny Italy.
And live the way befits a queen; a life of luxury.'
But Cleopatra's no one's fool, she knows him to be false,
And picks instead a harsher; a more fatalistic course.

Unto her bosom then she takes a deadly, biting asp.
And utters with her dying breath a last immortal gasp.
'So fare thee well. Now boast thee, death, in thy possession lies.' (Act

5, 1)
And with this final utterance Queen Cleopatra dies.

Thus, seeing how the asp has set her late employer free,
Sweet Charmian, her maid opines, 'that's good enough for me.'
She too takes up a deadly asp and holds it to her arm.
The asp of course obliges - and delivers deadly harm.

When Caesar sees before him this most awful tragedy,
He is overcome with grief and he issues a decree.
'To separate these two,' he says,' to me would be absurd.
For many years they've been as one, so should they be interred.'

Coriolanus

In ancient Rome there's discontent among plebeian folk.
The price of grain has gone sky high and that's no blooming joke!
'We want to set the price ourselves,' the common folk all shout.
So what then should the rulers do, to sort the problem out?

They devise a spiffing wheeze to keep the rebels quiet.
Five men to represent their views in the Roman diet.
But there's a famous soldier, Caius Martius is his name.
A man who's won a lot of wars and gained a deal of fame.

To see that common folk have won, fills him with discontent.
He looks upon the hoi polloi with loathing and contempt.
Then comes an urgent call to arms. It's off to war again.
As Caius Martius goes to Corioles with his men.

The leader of the Volscian tribe, Aufidius by name.
Is also one who over time has gained a lot of fame.
Though he's no match for Caius and the Romans have their way.
Tullus Aufidius will live to fight another day.

The battle now is over and it's time to head to Rome.
Where joyful citizens await, to welcome him back home.
The thrashing of the Volscians brings an increase to his fame.
As well as hugs and kisses he is given a new name.

He'll be known as Coriolanus from this moment on.
(A better name you'd have to say than Jimmy, Jack or John!)
The whole of Rome is cheering, even those he deems as scum.
And proudest of those cheering is Volumnia, his mum.

What next then for our hero? Well it's politics of course.

For he's a man that happily most Romans would endorse.
But kissing babes and shaking hands is something he'd abhor.
Especially if the hand he shakes, belongs to someone poor!

But Brutus and Sicinius; two senators of note,
Address the commoners of Rome and tell them, 'do not vote
For that man Coriolanus, who treats you with disdain.
Instead when polling day comes round, just vote for us again.'

The idea that the hoi polloi should have a vote at all,
Is something that quite frankly drives our hero up the wall.
'Be temperate,' his mother says,' and do what others do.
Tell them what they want to hear, even if it is untrue.'

He does what any son should do, he listens to his mum.
And cosies up, with great reluctance, to the city's scum.
But Brutus and Sicinius are most persuasive men.
And in the blinking of an eye, they win them back again.

With language most immoderate, he rails against the state.
It's enough on this occasion to seal the proud man's fate.
He leaves the ungrateful city, his wife and his old mum,
And goes to join his former foe, now lodged in Antium.

'I'm here to be your friend,' he says, 'and help in every way.
To go against my one-time pals and make the rotters pay.'
The former foes are now best friends and thus march off to war.
And very soon they find themselves outside Rome's city door.

'Oh spare us,' says Cominius, a senator of Rome.
'Don't put the city to the sword that used to be your home.'
His words all fall on stony ground; his pleas are brushed aside.
'No joy,' he tells his fellow Romans, 'but at least I tried.'

It seems that nothing in the world can stop the city's fall,
Until his mum, his wife and child, decide to pay a call.
They meet with Coriolanus. His mum lays down the law.
She tells him he's a naughty boy and thus prevents a war.

With his mother's disapproval still ringing in his ears,
He tells his Volscian followers to put away their spears.
And so in place of enmity, there's peace for years to come.
Which goes to show it's always right to listen to your mum!

The Volscians back in Antium are overcome with joy.
'Oh Coriolanus,' they cry, 'you're such a clever boy.
Now thanks to you the wasteful years of war and strife will cease.
You've made a truce twixt us and Rome and brought a lasting peace.'

But Aufidius is jealous and shares not in their joy.
To him the Roman general's nothing but a mummy's boy;
A mountebank, a Fancy Dan and treacherous to boot.
And if guns had been invented, someone he'd like to shoot.

With thoughts of retribution racing round inside his head,
Aufidius won't be satisfied until the Roman's dead.
With his cronies gathered round him, they form a deadly ring.
And then in swift succession each takes out his pointy thing.

They stab him in the abdomen. They stab him in the neck.
And do not cease their stabbing till he's dead upon the deck.
'What have you done, you foolish boys?' the Volscian elders shout.
'This man has brought us victory and now you've rubbed him out.'

As he gazes ruefully at the mangled, bloody corse,
Aufidius, his murderer, is filled up with remorse.
'A noble Roman's lying there,' he says through floods of tears.
'Whose name will live forever...or at least a few more years.'

Timon of Athens

In days of yore there lived a gent who had a load of cash.
He lent it here, he lent it there and did it with panache.
He threw parties for his neighbours and folk of every sort.
And everyone in Athens said, 'this man is such a sport.'

Popular as sun in winter, a brick, a proper gent.
But that soon changed the moment that his money all was spent.
For when he came to poverty, they liked not what they saw.
No one it seems will be his friend now he is church mouse poor.

Says Timon to his creditors, 'I need some time to pay.'
'No chance,' they all cry out as one, 'you must cough up today.'
It's Flavius, his serving man, who gets a bloody nose.
The poor man takes the blame for all of Timon's current woes.

No one will help poor Timon out when he requests a loan.
And so this one-time benefactor ends up all alone.
He holds one final party and once the guests are seated,
Serves each one a special treat of water slightly heated.

Alcibiades, in the meantime, down on bended knee,
Is pleading with the senators to let a soldier free.
'To hang this man,' he tells the senate, 'goes beyond the pale.'
But though he tries his very best, his pleas are doomed to fail.

Alcibiades, they concur, is nothing but a pain.
He's then instructed, 'go away and don't come back again.'

He meets up with old Timon; now a most unhappy man.
And living in a new abode, laid out as open plan.
Poor chap he has no money and his situation's grave.

How else could someone of his standing end up in a cave?

But then one day whilst rooting round for food upon the wold.
Our indigent unfortunate digs up a pot of gold!
Along comes Apemantus; a philosopher of sorts,
Who mocks him for his weakness, then about his find reports.

The news brings Alcibiades and pirates by the score,
Who form a queue outside the cave's imaginary door.
But Timon is a much changed man; a bitter man withal,
And he'd like nothing better than to see the city fall.

The cache he found beneath the ground, he'll offer as reward.
'There's gold for all,' he says, 'if you put Athens to the sword.

Alcibiades and his men get ready for the fray.
Then set out for the city, where they hope to win the day.
But there is small resistance from the folk of Athens town.
As in the twinkling of an eye they lay their weapons down.

The senators turn to Timon, to help them if he can.
But malcontented Timon has a far, far better plan.
'Go hang yourselves,' he tells them, ' I really do not care.
And if you do please use the tree outside my grotty lair.'

'Agree,' says Alcibiades, 'to the captives' release.
And in return I promise there will be enduring peace.'
And thus it is the senators; all cowards to a man.
Decide that they will fall in with Alcibiades plan.

A soldier then comes to the scene with tidings of great woe.
'I saw,' he tells the milling throng, 'a little while ago.
A tablet with great Timon's name - and written large thereon,
A message that would indicate the poor old fellow's gone.'

Here lie I, Timon, who alive all living men did hate. (Act 5,4)
(It seems he knew instinctively he'd passed his sell by date!)

The Romances

Pericles Prince of Tyre

John Gower tells the story.
Sometimes lewd, sometimes gory.
Of how the Prince of Tyre,
His belly full of fire,
Set sail to find a bride.

But to fulfil his wildest dreams,
Won't be as simple as it seems.
In Antioch across the water,
There's a king who has a daughter.
She's the one he'd like to wed.

But the king's a proper tease
And very, very hard to please.
He won't let his daughter travel,
Till somebody can unravel,
A riddle he's devised.

So Pericles applies his mind,
This tricky poser to unwind.
It's only then that he discovers,
The daughter and her dad are lovers,
And decides to leave the scene.

This oh so deadly revelation,
About familial fornication,
Could result in Pericles,
Being chopped off at the knees.
Making him and the play much shorter.

Back in Tyre still feeling restless,

He decides to sail to Tarsus.
Where ruler Cleon and his wife,
Are on the very edge of life.
There's no food at all around.

But Pericles distributes food,
And earns the nation's gratitude.
Having saved this seaside nation,
From the threat of dire starvation,
He sails off once again.

But the sea's a cruel master,
And his ship meets with disaster.
It sinks down to the ocean floor.
The prince is dumped upon the shore.
But all is not yet lost.

Three fishermen upon the strand,
Are there to give a helping hand.
They take him to the royal court,
Where there's a tourney being fought,
To celebrate a birthday.

The birthday in particular,
Is that of the young Thaisa.
She is the fairest in the land,
And Pericles would like the hand.
Of King Simonides' daughter.

To make the princess his by rights,
He must defeat the other knights.
Which he does with flashing blade,
And wins the lovely, royal maid.
They then sail off together.

And even though the weather's wild,
Thaisa gives birth to a child.
The baby's named Marina.
Thaisa dies before she's seen her,

And they bury her at sea.

Which seems a most unhappy ending.
But is she dead or just pretending?

Her coffin floats to Ephesus.
Pericles sails on to Tarsus.
Tarsus is the city where,
He leaves Marina in the care,
Of Cleon and Dionyza.

In Ephesus the coffin lands,
Upon the golden, sun-kissed sands.
Where it's discovered ere too long,
By good and honest Cerimon,
A doctor of renown.
With pills and portions that revive,
The dead girl's soon once more alive.

With breath restored you'd think she'd seize
The chance to be with Pericles.
But somewhere deep inside her head,
She's sure that Pericles is dead,
And makes a different choice.

Instead she takes the life most simple,
And dons a dress, topped by a wimple.
Her future days all now will be,
Filled up with prayer and chastity,
In the temple of Diana.

The scene now shifts to Myteline,
Where young Marina; aged fourteen,
Has newly been recruited,
By a house that's ill reputed.
Taken there by pirates
Who'd saved her from the envious knife,
Of Dionyza; Cleon's wife.

(It was her servant actually,
She hired to do the deed, not she.)
Marina's cuter than her daughter.
That's why she's planned the poor girl's slaughter...
A mother non-pareil!

Meanwhile the lonely Pericles,
Goes sailing round the open seas.
Until he reaches Tarsus town,
Where feeling low, his head hung down,
He hears the awful news
His daughter's passed away.
Which prompts poor Pericles to say,
That though he'll smell just like a drain,
He'll never wash or shave again.

A bawdy house in Mytilene,
Is where we set the final scene.
Lysimachus the local mayor,
Would like, if possible to share
Some time with sweet Marina.
But she, I think you all should know,
Is purer than the driven snow.
So they don't lie upon the bed,
They kneel down on the floor instead,
And say their prayers together.

Lysachimus is most impressed,
And takes her with him as a guest,
To a ship where sad Pericles,
Is getting sadder by degrees,
To try to cheer him up.

He hears her sing and though not sure,
He thinks he's heard her voice before.
Although it's years since he's seen her.
He concludes that it's Marina,
And gives the girl a hug.

They then sail on a balmy breeze,
To meet with Mrs Pericles.
(She with frumpy dress and wimple:
Lives inside Diana's temple.)
Lysimachus and Marina wed.
And now the two will share a bed.

The Pericles' are united.
And everybody is delighted.
Except for Cleon and his mate,
Who both have met an awful fate.

Cymbeline

King Cymbeline of Britain is mightily offended.
His daughter, Imogen, won't wed the man he intended.
His stepson Cloten is the one he wanted her to wed.
But she has picked a lowborn man called Posthumus instead.

Young Posthumus, though handsome, is a man of no estate,
No cash, no goods, no anything, though keen to be her mate,
The king decides the only way that he can put things right,
Is send poor Posthumus abroad, out of his daughter's sight.

It's in the land of Italy his exile is begun:
A land of wine and pasta bake and endless hours of sun.
Where after just a little while he meets Iachimo.
Iachimo's a wily one; a slipp'ry so and so.

The wily one tells Posthumus all women are the same.
To prove it he'll bed Imogen, to show she has no shame.
He heads for Britain straight away to do the evil deed.
But she's not that sort of girl and his plan does not succeed.

Iachimo is determined. He has a strategy.
Instead of giving up the chase, he operates plan B.
Inside a chest, beside her bed, while Imogen's asleep,
Iachimo climbs quietly out to have a little peep.

Now satisfied with what he's seen, Iachimo goes home.
And meets up with young Posthumus, deep in the heart of Rome.
He tells the exiled Posthumus, he knows she has a mole
Then shows him with alacrity a bracelet that he stole.

A bracelet given Imogen the day the two were wed.

So now he's filled with anger and just wants to see her dead.
To Pisanio, his servant, he sends a hate-filled note.
Telling him to kill her, bump her off, cut her throat.

He won't do it; he's been too long in Imogen's employ.
Instead he tells her, 'change your clothes and dress up as a boy.'
This done he tells young Posthumus, 'I've killed your lady wife.
I did exactly what you said. I stabbed her with a knife.'

Fair Imogen sets off at once to win her husband back,
But very soon discovers she's strayed off the beaten track.
She finds herself outside a cave in deepest, darkest Wales,
Where lives the duke, Belarius, with two more strapping males.
The first one's named Guiderius; the oldest of the pair.
The other Arviragus... all three share this rocky lair.

Sweet Imogen is welcomed in. They think she is a lad.
The clottish Cloten then turns up and he is hopping mad.
Mad Cloten and Guiderius soon get into a fight.
And though he fights with valour, Cloten's beaten out of sight.

Upset by all the aggro, Imogen surveys the scene,
And reaches for a calming potion, given by the queen.
Made drowsy by the potion she lays down her weary head.
To Belarius and his boys, it looks like she is dead.

Believing that their new found friend has gone to paradise,
They bear her off with heavy heart, to where dead Cloten lies.
But Imogen is still alive and when she comes around.
She sees the headless Cloten there beside her on the ground.
His corpse is dressed in finery like that her hubby wore
Small wonder then that Imogen is shaken to the core.

Meanwhile a Roman general comes demanding to be paid,
As per the binding contract, which with Cymbeline he'd made.
It's about protection money, to be paid to mighty Rome.
Which states that if he pays them cash, he'll stay safe in his home.

Imogen meanwhile has dressed herself as a lowly page.

And seeks a job with the Romans, to earn a living wage.
But Imogen is unaware that Posthumus is there:
That just like her he too has found a different garb to wear.

He's changed his stylish toga for a set of peasant's togs.
Weighed down by guilty feelings, he just wants to pop his clogs.
The Romans are defeated by the British on the day.
(It's cavemen one, the Romans nil... hip, hip, hip, hip hooray!)

To the court of Cymbeline, the prisoners are escorted.
(Let's face it there are many things still need to be sorted)
Imogen and Posthumus are united once again.
They then forgive Iachimo, who'd caused them so much pain.

Belarius tells Cymbeline, 'I took your boys from you.
Now I'd like to give them back: it's the decent thing to do.'
The king forgives Belarius, then lets the prisoners go.
And finally agrees to pay the Romans loads of dough.

A doctor then announces that the queen has passed away.
A neat and tidy ending to a complicated play.

A Winter's Tale

Bohemia's king Polixenes in Sicily has been.
With his friend the king Leontes and Hermione, his queen.
Polixines then tells the king, that though it breaks his heart,
He thinks he's been there far too long and now he must depart.

But pregnant queen Hermione, who has a lovely smile,
Persuades good King Polixines to linger for a while.
Which makes her hubby, Leontes, suspicious as can be.
Why he wonders has he listened to her and not to me?

Convinced his friend has been too close to wife Hermione.
His friendly feelings turn to rage and rampant jealousy.
He calls upon his confidant, the wise Lord Camillo.
And tells him in the strongest terms, 'that man has got to go.'

Camillo gets the gist of what his lord and master's said.
But does not kill Polixenes... he tips him off instead.
The pair then flee from Sicily as quickly as they can.
Which leaves the king Leontes a most embittered man.

The angry king Leontes, with his patience now outworn,
Throws his wife into a cell, where the little child is born.
Hoping for a change of heart when he sees the pretty thing,
Hermione's maid, Paulina, takes the baby to the king.

The king is not a bit impressed, he has already planned,
To have the child removed unto a far and distant land.
Not by her, but Antigonus, her hubby for some time.
Just he and he alone will carry out the awful crime.

No telephone or e-mail, so Leontes writes a note.
To the Oracle at Delphi, to see how she would vote.

Leontes asks the Oracle, 'How guilty is my wife?'
To which she says, 'She's innocent; so spare the lady's life.'

The judge and all the jury in the courtroom then agree,
Hermione must be innocent and so they set her free.
But there's no time to celebrate, sad news is on the way.
Her son, the brave Mamillius, has newly passed away.

The separation from his mum was far too much to bear.
And now he's in his grave, poor chap, beyond all pain and care.
It's too much for Hermoine; she too becomes a corse.
Which leaves the king, Leontes, full of sadness and remorse.

Antigonus meanwhile has landed on Bohemia's shore.
About to lay the baby down he hears a wild bear roar.
Its curtains for Antigonus; who's eaten by the bear.
So who is left to give the babe some tender loving care?

The answer to this question comes just half way through Act Three.
When a shepherd finds the foundling and renders TLC.
To protect the little baby from any further harm.
Together with his son he takes the child back to his farm.

Fast forward sixteen years or so... the baby's now become
A full-grown, nubile woman, who one day could be a mum.
The son of King Polixenes, the young Prince Florizel,
Adores a shepherd's daughter more than words could ever tell.

He sees her at a country fair while she is shearing sheep.
A sight he's never seen before that makes his young heart leap.
So smitten is young Florizel; his eyes fixed on the prize,
He fails to see Camillo and his father in disguise.

Autolycus, who earlier had pinched a shepherd's purse,
Is also at the fair, providing music song and verse.
Once the entertainment's over Polixenes reveals,
Unto the lovesick Florizel, exactly how he feels.

He tells him that the girl he's picked is not the one to wed.

That he should take to wife a girl of royal birth instead.
But aided by Autolycus, the couple quickly flee,
To the court of King Leontes in sunny Sicily.

Polixenes, Camillo and the shepherds follow on.
For a while the stage is empty with all the players gone.
So now it's time for Florizel to do the decent thing.
And introduce his love, Perdita, to the country's king.

Polixenes arrives at court his entourage around.
The shepherd then reveals how sweet Perdita first was found.
Of how the good Antigonus left the baby by the sea,
Until a bear came on the scene and had him for his tea.

When King Leontes hears the news Perdita is his child:
The tiny baby he himself had ruthlessly exiled,
He's overcome with gratitude and feelings of regret.
But our play is not quite over ... it gets much stranger yet.

Outside there is a statue of Hermione, his late wife,
Which knocks the socks off everyone by coming back to life.
Leontes welcomes back his wife... he wants to make amends.
Perdita and Prince Florizel get married in the end.

Camillo weds Paulina and they all go on their way.
The Winter's Tale is over and true love has won the day.

The Tempest

A sun-drenched island far away,
Is where Will sets his final play.
Upon this isle there lives a man,
The rightful Duke of old Milan.
Who by his sibling, spurred by greed,
Was cast upon the open sea.
'T was Antonio, his brother.
Foul Alonso was another,
Who cast poor Prospero adrift
And left him feeling rather miffed.

With his daughter, young Miranda, they drifted on awhile.
Until they came upon this far and distant, magic isle.
Where dwelt the spirit Ariel and fearsome Caliban:
Son of Sycorax, the witch, he's partly beast, partly man.

And then upon a certain day, when twelve long years had passed.
There's seen upon the ocean wide a heaving galleon's mast.
On board the ship are those who took his rightful throne away.
Now with the use of magic, Prospero will spoil their day.

He summons up a tempest, which rends the ship asunder.
Then sends it to the ocean floor, several fathoms under.
The wretched travellers one and all come finally to land.
Among them king of Naples and his son Prince Ferdinand.

With gentle music Ariel doth Ferdinand beguile.
Then leads him to Miranda, somewhere deep within the isle.
When she claps eyes on Ferdinand, she's shaken to the core…
Apart from pa Miranda's never seen a man before!

Meanwhile the king of Naples seeks a friendly, helping hand
To find out what has happened to the missing Ferdinand.
He seeks help from Sebastian, who's brother to the king.
An evil man who has in mind a very naughty thing.

Antonio, usurper; current duke of all Milan,
Asks Sebastian to kill the king, quickly as he can.
But Ariel; invisible unto the human eye,
Awakes the king with music and the plot goes all awry.

Stephano, a drunken butler and jester Trinculo,
Share a beer with Caliban, who wants rid of Prospero.
But as before good Ariel hears every word that's said.
And straightway lets his master know the monster wants him dead.

To celebrate his daughter's wedding to Prince Ferdinand,
A banquet in the grandest style by Prospero is planned.
Aware that Caliban et al, still pose an ugly threat,
Prospero decides to show them how horrid things can get.

To demonstrate what happens when such people misbehave,
He tells the sprightly, Ariel, 'Go bring them to my cave.'
It's there he tempts them with a set of brightly coloured togs.
Then has them chased by spirits, that turn into rabid dogs.

He next confronts Antonio and tells him man to man.
'I'm your brother, Prospero, rightful duke of all Milan.'
He then rebukes Sebastian, who'd planned to kill the king.
(Who else but a bounder would ever think of such a thing?)

Now we've reached the final scene, but before he goes to sea.
Prospero sets his servants, Caliban and Ariel free.
He breaks his staff of magic and departs the island's shore,
To rule the dukedom of Milan, as in the days of yore.